TERVEIN

There is a saying that the man dies, his soul stays earlier around the body and then in and around the house and watches keenly about the relations and their thinking and life after his death for thirteenth days. On thirteen day so called ' Tervein' the soul gets ready to travel to the other loka a world called the world of Lord Yama the god of death to get its judgement depending upon its Karma of the past.

This is the story based on the saying whereby the soul of Zamindar stays in and around the village and even travels outside to see what happens to his mother, wife and other relatives when he was alive and unaware of their existence. The entire matter of its stay described – as adventure of soul after death was narrated by him to the only dalit of the village whom he always described as untouchable. However he narrated his adventures to him knowing that no body will believe him if this dalit ever talks about zamindar's soul telling about its adventures. On thirteenth day after the panditji and relatives performed the rituals of 'Tervein' the soul left to the other world and the same event witnessed by dalit who thought that in the other world if the judgment by Lord Yama is given on bases of ones karma and not on caste, creed and richness then why not do good karma and not worry about the people of this physical world.

Dr. Krishna Rajvir, M.S., FRACS, MNAMS, FICS, is presently a senior Paediatric Surgery Consultant at Apollo Hospital, New Delhi. She had her training in general and paediatric surgery at various hospitals in Australia. She was the first Asian woman to get an FRACS in surgery and become a member of the Royal Australian College of Surgeons and a member of the Paediatric Association of Australia. On her return, she worked at the Post-graduate Institute of Medical Education and Research, Chandigarh as clinician, teacher and medical researcher. She has written books in her own specialty and has to her credit over 147 scientific papers published in national and international medical journals. She is also the chief editor of the Journal of Paediatric Surgery in Developing Countries.

Her interest in the women in feudal India started during her first visit to a remote village in Uttar Pradesh and this followed the writing of her book *The Zamindar's Bahu*- the first non-scientific book of her career, others are *Janams, Kailash the abode of Shiva* and *The second wife.*

She can be contacted at krishna.yadav@rvsyfoundation.org

Tervein

Krishna Rajvir

Dev Books

Dedicated to

Raj Vir Singh Yadav

Published by

DEV BOOKS

11-B Court Road

Delhi 110 054

Ph: 98102 36140

email:devbooks@hotmail.com

www.devbooks.co.in

ISBN 10: 81–89835–08–4

ISBN 13: 978-81–89835–08–8

First published 2009

Printed in India

Contents

The Funeral

THE DEAD body was waiting to be cremated. It was 11 a.m. in the morning, twenty hours and seven minutes to be exact, had passed since the death occurred. Though the ancient, ancestral mango grove was dense and every tree was laden with unripe fruits, the weather was hot and sultry except for an occasional cool breeze from the north. In spite of the unbearable weather, the gathering of over three hundred or so men, young and old, who sat on the dusty uneven sandy ground in front of the unlit pyre was quiet. The silence engulfed the entire surroundings. It appeared as if the fear of the man, even in death, cast a shadow over them.

Ramia, the local Dalit, sat in one corner of the grounds away from the others. He came in spite of the anger in his family; of his frail half-starved wife and his son, against the practice of untouchability by the local people under the rule of the zamindar. Even after twenty years of independence, this practice was still followed. Moreover, the dead man till his last breath was a staunch believer in untouchability and authoritatively demanded that the Dalit family in the village should work on a meagre salary and live as untouchables in the village without complaining to the local officers in tehsil Kaurali. This was despite being aware of the law of the nation, that it was a crime to even call someone an untouchable and the punishment for this was imprisonment up to three years.

No one in the gathering had eaten since the body was laid on the wooden pyre during the early hours of the morning. None of the men and women of the village worked that day. So the cooking pots at home were empty and would remain so till the dead man was cremated in accordance with the religious rituals, so that the soul was satisfied before its departure to the other land.

The old man was unlike his great grandparents and father. Chaudhary Mohan Singh was known as the lion of village Mauli in Uttar Pradesh. He lay ill – neither alive nor dead – for the last four days, but was now dead as certified by the vaid. Religious rituals were performed and the body was brought to the ancestral grounds for cremation.

He lay on the white cotton sheet, on the freshly made wooden pyre, erected under the same mango tree where his forefathers and father were cremated. It was sad that none of these rich people ever thought of constructing a permanent platform exclusively in the zamindar's family name, Mauli. The men were sitting still and those who moved did so silently. Death visits everyone, rich or poor, young or old, so suddenly. And so it did to Chaudhary Mohan Singh, but with a difference, as compared to an ordinary person living in the village. He died with his stomach and his treasury full. These were bad times for an ordinary man, because everything was expensive and prices, even for simple food, were soaring.

Sitting alone, holding a matchbox in his right hand, Ramia thought, 'One is better dead than alive.' Even for the dead man it was not easy these days. He got less respect from the younger generation. The two women in the haveli had made the Chaudhary's life miserable. Sumitra, his grandmother, was so dominating that at times it was unbearable. The old man was lucky to die. It was his misfortune to die when his only son was away. He wondered what would be his own fate, more so if his wife, Chunia, left him.

The mere thought of the younger generation – his son, Rajan, and daughter-in-law, Gudia, made him shake. However, he was confident that his son would perform the required rituals at his death, if only to show the local people that he was a loving and responsible heir to his father's assets. He admired the village panchayat for being strict about performing all the religious rituals during and after the death of any member of the village of Mauli.

The naked truth of his tethered life made him smile within himself. He knew this would teach his daughter-in-law a lesson – she who constantly called him a miser, hiding his valuables, not sharing them with his son's family. The small tin box, locked and placed under his bed was in the eye of the family. Even his wife, ever the chatterbox, who could not be trusted to remain quiet, wondered, but she never dared to touch the box or to ask him.

He looked at the dead body lying so helpless in such sultry weather. The zamindar who never worked in his life, survived the turmoil of the sudden abolition of the zamindari in 1957, raised his son and daughter with dignity and in comfort. He was not very kind or honest. He roared like a lion and yet earned the respect of the entire village. Ramia looked at the body, then at the mango tree shading it and wondered about the dead man's soul. The thought of the living soul of such a man looking at him made him shiver and the matchbox he held felt heavy.

Looking at the dead man, he reminisced: 'One should have seen this man in his youth – the only son of the rich and powerful zamindar, who owned over twenty villages during the colonial Raj. He was short, but had a masculine body. His large piercing globe-like eyes on a fair-complexioned broad face, covered with a huge moustache haunted those he disliked. In his early youth, he was a playboy. He loved women and wine and was fond of gambling. He never studied; spent his time teasing the village maidens, even hurting them physically; and taming the wild cows (neelgai) to drive his buggy instead of horses. He even reared lion cubs to scare the villagers. He hunted all day long with his few friends, being a voracious meat eater, but he was a miser to his core, unlike his father.

'Once he took a sanyas.' The very thought of that incident brought a smile to Ramia's lips. He thanked his bushy moustache for shielding this unaccountable act. 'The young master, wearing a long saffron robe, built a temple (a small brick pedestal) with his friends in the field next to the well. He placed the local gram devta inside at an auspicious time and date as advocated by the family priest. For the next three days, he and the others chanted mantras in praise of Lord Shiva, drank milk mixed with bhang and ate dhatura ladoos. However, when he failed to please Lord Shiva or get his darshan, he threw the Shivlingam into the tube well nearby and walked home as an atheist, never to enter a temple again.'

He looked at the dog, the shiny black animal called Shera sitting next to the unlit pyre. He wondered, 'The loyalty of this animal!' The creature never left his side while he was alive and now sat next to the unlit pyre. 'How loyal, and that too for a master who only gave him his discarded meat-free-bones and dry chapattis and kept him at home by his side as his slave – just like me,' Ramia thought, with a sarcastic laugh.

The sudden screech of tyres brought life to the morose gathering. It was an old jeep from the zamindar's house. A young man, who had not yet seen his thirtieth year, wearing a dhoti and vest, stepped out holding the hand of a three-year-old boy. Taking quick steps, he reached the pyre. He uncovered his father's face, and for a moment was lost in his own emotions. The child kissed his grandfather's hand and talking in his childish way, he placed a toffee in the dead man's hand. The child was hurriedly taken away. The people sitting there wondered about the child! No one knew that the man was married, because he did not live in Mauli, and the child was already three years old! However, many smiled to themselves, knowing well the reputation of that haveli.

The family priest chanted mantras while the local barber shaved the head of the dead man's son but not of the boy. That was unusual for those who were there! If he was the grandson then why was his hair not shaved? The priest signalled to Ramia, who stepped towards the unlit pyre. A special passage was created for him, because no one wanted to be touched. The young man took the matchbox from Ramia, gave him a five-rupee note and turned to light the pyre. This was an old ritual of the village, whereby the presence of a Dalit was a necessity, irrespective of whether the dead person was poor or rich. The pyre was lit amidst the chanting of mantras, the pouring of ghee and the placing of sandalwood sticks. Everyone waited till the ritual was over, at around mid-afternoon. The villagers paid their last farewell and then wended their way to the village well next to the grove for their purifying ritual bath. The very close relatives and friends of the dead man went to the haveli. Their entry, brought, a loud spell of weeping from the women gathered in the zenana. Then suddenly there was silence.

It was a long time since anyone had eaten any food. The fire was lit in the kitchen and the cooks, specially called for the occasion, prepared the simple food. They all ate, and so did the family priest, to his heart's content. Suddenly there was no shadow of death.

Gujral Singh, the dead man's son placed a hundred-rupee note in the Brahmin's palm. The Brahmin looked at the note, at the future heir, then at the bundles containing rice, lentils and finally at the sky and said softly, 'The soul of the departed zamindar is not happy. You must add some gold.' The dead man's wife came up to him, took off her gold ring and gave it him. The priest then, dipped some mango leaves into the holy Ganga water and sprinkled it on her forehead chanting mantras. All the women gathered in the house now surrounded him in order to be purified by the same ritual, paying five to ten rupees to have the water sprinkled on their heads. The son came forward to escort the priest to the gate, where Ramia was still waiting for his food.

'Has my father taken birth somewhere?' the new zamindar asked.

'Not yet,' the Brahmin replied, touching his sacred thread, 'it will happen after the tervein ceremony, on the thirteenth day after the cremation. After the ritual of the thirteenth day the soul will leave this house and undertake the journey to Yama's land. The future outcome, whether he goes to narak or heaven or stays in pitra loka or will be reborn depends on his karma.'

'My father will go to heaven like my grandfather?'

'Yes!' The Brahmin decided to be diplomatic as he was a resident of the same village.

Ramia wondered at God's discretion. He thought that if the rich and the poor, a Brahmin and a Dalit are the same in God's house and birth after death is not based on money, status, a high caste or creed on this earth, but on one's karma, then why worry about life after death! The sound of his name from a member of the house to collect the leftover food sickened him for the first time. He got up and without looking back left the house. For the first time in his life, he held his head high and walked erect, because from now he wanted to live free with dignity, even under the shadow of naked poverty but away from the chains of untouchability, humility and fear of the rich and powerful, who dared to discard an untouchable, a Dalit, and give him leftovers to eat.

Taking quick steps on the kutcha, uneven, narrow road, both sides of which had open drains that gave off a putrid smell, he walked fast, almost running, to get away from the shadow of the zamindar's haveli, to his house on the outskirts of the village, marked out for Dalits.

A firm but hoarse voice made him turn. There was nobody. He wondered who it could be! The voice was familiar but he continued taking hurried steps. A soft pressure on his left shoulder and his name taken again with so much authority made him stand still; the fear of the dead man's soul roaming around in the village alarming him. He remembered the Brahmin's words that soul would hover around the haveli for thirteen days. The voice was the zamindar's! It shook him from head to toe. His face turned pale and his body had no energy to take another step. A spell of giddiness made him too sick to move, so he sat under the old pipal tree next to the village pond. Holding his head with both hands he wondered about the reason for this spell. It could be fear of the dead man's soul, hovering around the village, hunger, anxiety, or the fight he had with his wife, who was reluctant to allow him to attend the funeral. She wanted to leave the village when his older son left for Mumbai but stayed back because of him. 'Silly woman,' he thought.

He remembered his recent fight with his younger son Raja who showed no concern for his parents, except to extract the money he earned occasionally from the zamindar's house and his small piece of land. The very thought of the younger generation being so disrespectful, uncaring and selfish brought a mist in front of his eyes. He wished he had no children, feeling he would have been better off living alone with his wife, without having a daily feud with his son and daughter-in-law. The older son too, had not written or visited the village since he left.

There was a sudden silence, even the birds stopped chirping. He looked around the pond, at the houses, the narrow kutcha lanes with their filthy drains and at the haveli. Nothing had changed – the local people of the village or the haveli, whether it was the Raj of the Mughals, the English or the National Government. The thought of his love for his land of birth made him smile inside and suddenly he felt better.

He laid himself on the stone pavement built by Chaudhary Mohan Singh's great grandfather, closed his eyes and decided to relax before going home. He wanted to think of an explanation to give his ailing wife as to why he had not brought the leftover food from the haveli. He was still debating when he felt someone sit by his left side.

He kept his eyes closed and waited but for some time there was no sound. Then there was a movement and the sound of a pebble thrown into the pond. He was sure none of his grandchildren could have come looking for him. He opened his eyes and looked around. There was nobody. He remembered the words of the priest – the soul will leave the house and the village on the thirteenth day. Suddenly he stood up and decided to leave, to enter the security of his hut, because he knew the soul would not enter a Dalit's house and specially that of the zamindar, who never wished to be touched by a Dalit and even took a bath in the sacred Ganga water after visiting the English Collector at Kaurali.

This thought satisfied him and gave him courage. He turned to leave but sat down again like a statue when the voice said, 'Ramia don't leave, I am alone and very sad as I can't talk to anyone. I wish to be with you because I want to spend the next thirteen days in peace and contentment and enjoy life as an unknown shadow who can see, hear and feel, but cannot be seen. You're the only one who will be with me and no one in the village will believe you if you tell them after my departure. They all know that my soul could not even talk to you, Ramia the Dalit and untouchable.'

Ramia listened carefully and then asked what he should do.

'First, return to my haveli, my young daughter Rani, still has the food for you. I remember the incident when you saved her from the mad bull running around in the village. She was only seven years old then, but she never forgot the sacrifice you made for her. I knew she gave you money, old clothes, sweets and even medicine for your wife without the family's knowledge. That tin box of yours still has the gold chain she gave you last Diwali.

'However, I also remained indebted to you and that was the reason I allowed only your family to stay on my land on the outskirts of the village, and gave you land. My resentment against Dalits was only to show the local people and the pandits who were not happy with your presence in the haveli and the money given to you occasionally. I also gave you the hathi khana (elephant house) to look after my elephant so that I could pay you more. I did all this because in my heart I knew you were an honest Dalit and faithful in times of need.

'I know you are hungry and so is your wife Chunia. She has fever, but is restless due to hunger. She asked your son to give her food but his wife, Gudia, refused and told her to wait for the leftovers from the haveli. The daughter-in-law's words were so curt that Chunia went inside her hut and closed the door. She didn't open it even when your son came with fresh chapattis and vegetables.'

The thought of his sick wife made Ramia get up and he walked towards the haveli even forgetting that he had learnt all this from the soul of the dead lion. His only aim was to get some food and go home to be with his wife. 'Children,' he thought and spat on the ground. For the first time he decided not to share any of his possessions with his son and his family, and to live separately in his hut with his wife.

The First Day

CHUNIA WAS SITTING at the door waiting for him, when he returned home late in the evening. He entered the house. It had two rooms but one was given to his son and his family. Recalling what the soul told him, he took a deep sigh and felt distressed at the behaviour of his son's family. He remembered how after getting a meagre amount of money, leftover food and old clothes from the haveli, they both worked in the zamindar's hathi khana for extra money and then on the small piece of land at times toiling till late in the evenings, to make ends meet. He did that in order to live with a happy and contended family. He was proud of his two sons and was convinced they would look after their parents in their old age. What a hope! He gave a cynical laugh and placed his possessions on the floor that Chunia had plastered so well with cow dung. He recalled his only other possession, Leela, the cow, now old enough to provide milk, but she too required food for a good yield. Chunia hardly ever kept any milk for him and always fed the grandchildren. He wondered why.

The thought of the son's family occupying his premises and their behaviour with his wife made his blood boil. He sat on the ground. There was too little water to bathe and he couldn't bathe at the village well because Dalits were not allowed to do so. He took a mug of water went outside, washed his hands and face and after wiping them came in and changed his torn dhoti.

Meanwhile, Chunia had served the food on a banana leaf and was waiting for him to eat first. She looked anxious, and no sooner did he start eating, then she told him, how Gudia had cooked food. But on asking for it, she not only refused, but bluntly told her to wait for Baba to come home with the leftovers. This angered her and she went into her room and locked the door.

'Yes! I know,' Ramia said without thinking.

'You know?'

'Yes.'

'But how?'

Ramia realized his mistake and to cover his statement he told her that he had observed Gudia's behaviour for several days. They ate their food and then she opened the bundle Rani had given her. It had a ten-rupee note, a cotton sari and a dhoti for Ramia.

There was silence as both thought about Rani and how, ever since he had saved her from the mad bull she took every opportunity to give them something on her visits to the haveli. He wondered how she fared in her in-laws' house. The only daughter of a rich zamindar married to a zamindar of equal status in another village, but her husband, Ram Singh, turned out to be a womanizer and loved wine and gambling. She returned home and stayed for some years with her parents, but went back when her in-laws asked her to and promised to look after her.

Poor girl, though she was the beloved daughter of a zamindar, with the entry of her stepmother everything changed and she was not happy in the haveli even though the Sahib loved her dearly and kept an eye on his wife. He was lost in thought when Chunia asked about news from the haveli.

'What news?'

'How is Rani?'

'She is well, a little thin but she has no children, and with her stepmother around and her father dead, she looked unhappy.'

Chunia heaved a deep sigh and put the clothes into the wooden box, the family's only other valuable possession. She placed the money in a small paper bag and knew that it now contained fifty rupees. Ramia didn't give her his five-rupee note because he knew that Chunia's money would be given to their son when he sweet-talked his mother.

It was now dark, so they decided to lie down without lighting the gas lantern. It was the same in the rest of the village. This was not the only village without electricity. It was 1970, yet there was no electricity in the village, not even in the haveli, but at least the rich could light up the entire palace with gas chandeliers, which was done daily, and the zamindar's palace, at a higher altitude looked down at the poor dwellings of the people of its zamindari!

Ramia came out and looked around, there were very few lights in the village but the haveli was the same and he wondered why it was so well lit when the master was not even dead for twenty hours. It was not so when Chaudhary Devi Singh died. His son, Mohan Singh had the haveli lit with a minimum of lights, and it was almost in darkness for the entire thirteen days. The same was ordered in the village and no one was allowed to play music or entertain in Mauli. They all abided by this order, even though there was no zamindari after the abolition of landlords in August 1957. Today, the young master stays away from Mauli in Lucknow, and has no say over the women.

Shaking his head with disappointment he entered the hut. Chunia was lying on the floor, half asleep. He took his place next to her and closed his eyes. It was very hot; he rose and opened the small window. What he saw took his breath away. It was a full moon night. The night of puranmashi and the silvery moon lit up the entire village and even his hut was flooded with light. A cool breeze started, he went back to his room and lay on the mat to sleep. However, his thoughts kept churning. A death on puranmashi was a good omen.

He knew Chaudhary Mohan Singh was his age. They were born on the same day, one in a Dalit family and the other in a rich, royal house. He remembered how his own grandmother, Prulia, dominated the entire village. Being the only midwife in Mauli, she was also close to the haveli. Ramia remembered how one night she narrated the incident of his birth. She had to go to the haveli because the zamindarin was in labour. Everyone was worried about the lady because even after five years of marriage, there was no heir. There were whispers about female infanticide, but the gossip remained with the villagers as none dared to ask Prulia the midwife, why one after the other the female babies died. His grandmother never spoke and the locals were scared to ask or annoy her. Even a word in the ears of the zamindar would mean severe punishment, because he had never bothered about either the British or the national government. He was the ruler of Mauli and remained so even after August 15, 1947 when the Congress Government took over from the British.

She was busy with the preparations for the delivery when Prulia was told in a whisper that her daughter-in-law was in labour. She was upset but knew that she couldn't go home. It was a difficult delivery, so the zamindarin was taken to Lucknow. The boy was born at Lucknow on the same day. To her horror she saw her daughter-in-law had delivered a boy and the baby with the cord was lying in a pool of blood and water from the womb. At first she thought both were dead but then all went well.

She did not want the zamindar to know that a son was born in a Dalit home on the same day as his heir was. So she asked all the five Dalit families to be silent about the birth and to make it more stringently secret, she started giving the baby opium. However, she called the baby Ramia, the baby who was saved by Lord Rama.

Ramia survived, but he lost his mother within a fortnight because of an infection in the womb, and the father drowned to death a month later, while crossing the local river of Mauli at midnight. Prulia earned enough, so she brought Ramia up. She built a two-room house and stayed in the village even when the other Dalit families left for Mumbai in the hope of a better future. In time to come, Ramia lost his grandmother and he was the only Dalit in the village.

He married and had two sons, and when Prulia died, owing to the lack of money and having to care for the family, Ramia was forced to take on more work. It was the young zamindar, Mohan Singh, who gave him work in the house and the hathi khana. They had to cook large chapattis for the big animal and bathe him daily. Both Chunia and Ramia started working in the haveli besides the small patch of land bought by his grandmother. There was a school in the village, but his sons were not allowed to study with the children of the other locals.

Both boys helped their father but as they grew up they became anti-feudal. The older son married Rampyari, a barber's daughter, and left for Mumbai, but the younger one stayed with Ramia. He was happy with his younger son but that changed within a year of his marriage to Gudia of Sarsa village. The boy became a barber in Kaurali and started earning money, but never helped his parents. He stayed with his family in the village and lived off his parents. Chunia loved her younger son, so would not allow Ramia to talk to him, but slowly both of them decided to ask him and his family to leave their house, so that they could live in peace during their old age. He was sure that the boy would perform their last rites to hide his shame and to grab their meagre assets – a little money, the house and the land. After today's incident, Chunia was determined to ask them to leave.

He continued thinking about the soul, through Chunia's snoring; there was no sleep. Then he heard the howling of a wolf and knew he had to go out. He took his mat and went out. He spread it on the stone platform and lay down. The moon was under a patch of cloud but the rest of the sky was studded with stars. The breeze was cool and gentle. He fell into deep slumber and all was forgotten.

The noise of the gentle opening of a door and footsteps awakened him and he looked around. He saw a shadow entering the barn. He stayed where he was and watched. After almost ten minutes he saw a woman coming out with a container. Suddenly, there was light as the moon came out from behind the patch of clouds. It was Gudia. He now realized why the cow yielded such a little milk in the mornings. He decided to keep this secret, but was more determined than ever to throw his son's family out of his house. He went to sleep again, thinking about his daughter-in-law's unsavoury behaviour. He fell asleep again, knowing that he was not only physically, but also emotionally tired. He covered himself with his torn sheet and fell into a deep sleep.

'Ramia,' the whisper awakened him. He kept lying down, holding his breath, to avoid the hoarse, thick voice but then he felt as though someone was sitting besides him. He couldn't control his breath and started coughing. As the cough stopped the voice whispered in his left ear, 'Ramia get up.'

'Who are you?' Ramia asked, pretending ignorance.

'Get up,' the voice was forceful and the way the words were spoken made Ramia sit up.

'The voice has the same command as when the lion was alive,' he thought. 'Even in death he is a terror!' There was a silence, then the whisper returned.

'I wish to talk to you and share my secrets and adventures in this village for the next thirteen days till I leave and never return to my birthplace.'

The word 'share' shook Ramia, and even though the weather was cool he started sweating.

'Wipe the sweat off your face and listen to me.'

'All right, but do you want something to eat or drink from a Dalit's house?'

'No, I am a soul, I can fly, sit, listen, read and talk, but am unable to hurt or hold or touch anyone. I live on smell, so don't worry about it. Now let me tell you what I saw during the first twenty-four hours after my death.' Ramia waited.

***

Chaudhary Mohan Singh's First Day as a Soul

Ramia, when the body was laid on the wooden pyre I was on the branch of the mango tree giving me shade, and which years ago had given shade to my parents and great grandparents. I saw that every male member of the village had come; they were sitting quietly, and you were alone in one corner holding your matchbox.

I looked at my dog, Shera, sitting close to me, yet I couldn't give him a loving stroke. They were all waiting but my son and grandson had not yet come.

Don't look so surprised, Ramia, the boy is my grandson but only my son and I knew. The marriage was kept secret to save his wife, Nirmala, and his son. That was also the reason why the family lived in Lucknow. My grandson is now three. People were getting restless waiting in the heat, but I was not in discomfort. When my son came and exposed my body I saw my cold, blue, hideous old body almost eaten up by the infection, even though the illness lasted only two weeks. However, all the years of torture were eating me from within. The sight of my body made me sick and I was glad that I would be free of pain and the effort of keeping my body protected and comfortable.

The pyre was lit and halfway through the burning, the priest pierced my skull to avoid a mishap – a tantric or witch-hunting man trying to capture me. I waited and observed everyone. One by one they left my burning pyre, excepet my son, cousins and close family relatives who came from outside. They were waiting for the pyre to cool down. I looked at the dog and saw that he was lying quietly, but there were tears in his eyes. I found my son in deep thought and I wanted to console him, but I was helpless.

Yes! I was helpless today as on the day when he wanted to marry Nirmala at Mauli and I told him not to, because of the two women in the haveli. Unlike the other zamindars of the family, the marriage was performed at Lucknow. I saw my grandson for the first time after my death. However, no one in the haveli knows even today that he married with my consent.

You know Ramia, the dog is an animal that has a sixth sense. I frequently saw him looking at the mango tree but Shera never barked. The pyre was almost cold, so I left the men there and went to the village well.

They were bathing to purify themselves and some of them were humming bhajans but the aura of the fear of death was all around. The human being can never control his tongue, and that was the scene there. Some were praising me in comparison to my father, Chaudhary Devi Singh, while others were sad that I died even before I was fifty. Some were talking about my son's arrogance and disrespect, till I felt sick. One person, the young bania, commented on my daughter-in-law, it was said in a whisper and they laughed. I couldn't hear what was said, but I was convinced it was about her character and not in her favour. Yes! The reputation of us zamindars with nautch girls made them laugh. However, I was helpless to defend Nirmala. There was some talk about the young child also. It will now be the gossip of Mauli. They bathed and walked swiftly to their homes to eat because it was past 4 p.m. and they were hungry.

I returned to the grove to see my son performing the last rites when Ram Dass, my personal servant, whispered something in his ear. They all bent down around the dog. Yes! He was dead. I felt sad but had no means to convey my feelings.

My son, Gujral Singh, asked Ram Dass to dig a grave under the tree and then both of them buried the animal while the priest chanted mantras and sprinkled Ganga water on the body of the animal. I wanted to hug my son for this kind gesture and thought that he was not as bad as people tried to make out – those who tried their best to keep us apart – those two women in the haveli. However, during the last four years we have been close to each other.

The men started walking towards the haveli and I sat on the windowsill of the sitting room. They bathed, ate to their heart's content and then for some time slept on the white sheets spread out on the floor of the hall. All were satisfied at the end of the ritual. I think no one wanted to remember my burning pyre and wished to leave as soon as possible. At times one wonders: you love the body when it is alive, but in death you wish to dispose of it as soon as possible. Why?

I saw you leave the haveli. I went to your house and found Chunia in tears as I told you. Then I returned to my pyre. Ram Dass was there to keep watch and ensure that nobody picked up or stole the bones which were not completely burnt. Ram Dass was sad, because he knew that he had lost me and with me his job. He knew that my son always blamed him for the gossip from the haveli leaking out to the locals. However, now he knew his value. I wanted to tell him not to worry, because I had left enough money for him with Gujral Singh when he came to the haveli to visit me.

I stayed there and wondered what to do next. That was when I got the idea that I could go on an adventure and look around for the buried secrets of the haveli and the locals and then share them with you. Ramia I always found you to be honest and faithful. So I decided to choose you as my companion during these thirteen days! It will be fun.

I sat on the branch of the mango tree and Ram Dass and I remained there till the full moon rose. A sudden doubt entered my mind and I knew why Ram Dass was there, even when Gujral Singh told him to get his food and ask someone else to keep an eye on the pyre till the pierced skull and bones could be collected in the morning. I also watched, because I knew that my broken skull would be used to capture my soul, keep it under control and get all the wretched work done by the witchcraft performed on me. This was the best night for black magic and every tantric works hard because it is more successful during the night of puranmashi.

I kept a watch even after Ram Dass went to sleep. Exactly at midnight there was a noise and I saw a figure in a white sari approach. She went up to Ram Dass and confirmed that he was asleep. Then she circled the pyre three times in the clockwise direction and four times in the anticlockwise direction. Suddenly, she took off her sari. I felt shame and closed my eyes but when I opened them, what I saw almost made me shout. It was the young sadhu, the ghori, who came sometimes to the village but was always driven away. I discovered that he had settled on the mound just above the cremation ground of village Sarsa, next to the river, which was once under us. He was almost naked now and started chanting and spreading my ash all over his body. Then he stirred the ash and started looking for something. It was so clearly seen under the light that he smiled when he got my partially broken skull. He placed a kiss on it and then started reciting. I got a feeling of being pushed into the body of a man.

It alarmed me, so I went close to Ram Dass and whispered his name. Ram Dass got up and flashed a torch at the man, who got up and was about to run away. But Ram Dass caught him and forced him to throw the skull back on the pyre. He then started beating the man till he almost lost consciousness. The moment the skull fell on the pyre I recovered my strength and resumed my seat on the branch.

As both of us watched the skull, the ghori sneaked away, but Ram Dass was relaxed and knew what to do with this sadhu in the morning. Men's voices could now be heard. There were three of them – my son, Gujral Singh and my uncle's son and nephew. They flashed a light and Ram Dass told them the story. My son looked very upset and angry. He wanted to take his revenge and teach the ghori a lesson. The gas lantern was lit, they placed the bones in the basket and then left the pyre. I followed them up to the haveli but then turned to be with you because it was almost after midnight.

'Ramia tell me about the ghori,' the voice said.

***

'They are usually of a low caste like me, but they eat meat, drink and even partake of the meat of dead humans. They pray with the skulls of dead people, mostly unpierced, but even pierced, as long as it is not completely broken. They often succeed in capturing a soul within the first thirteen days after death. This soul works according to their orders and is never allowed to go to Lord Yama's land. The soul becomes a bhut, when after thirteen days it acquires its physical form. The ghori cult does this to attract women who wish to take revenge or are barren. They sometimes make them steal young children, kill them and drink their blood. However, most of the time, they have sex with these women devotees, after doping them with drugs mixed into the prashad.'

'Ramia,' the voice said.

It alarmed Ramia because Chunia was up and standing by his side saying, 'Get up and help me. It is not yet dawn but I wish to milk the cow to get some milk for you. You have a bad habit of talking in your sleep and I wonder why you are talking about devotees and prashad mixed with drugs.'

'You start and I will come to help you,' Ramia replied. When Chunia left, he whispered, 'I must go.'

'Yes! We will meet tomorrow and I shall talk to you about my adventure of the second night.'

'Of course,' Ramia got up and with a smile bent down to fold his sheet. Somehow he now felt happy to be with the soul, and that too for another twelve days.

The Second Day

'RAMIA GET UP,' the voice made him open his eyes and he looked around. The sky was clear, the stars were scattered on the pale blue carpet of the sky, but there was no breeze. He sat up on the torn sheet the voice said, 'I am tired but I have to share my agony of the second day as a soul on this earth with you. Let me regain my breath, so please wait and then listen carefully.

***

I left you before the early dawn set in and headed towards the haveli but then stopped when a figure covered from head to foot in white came out from behind the door of the zenana meant for male servants, when they are required for some strenuous work. First I thought it must be a man but then looking closer I was surprised to see the figure of a woman clad in a white sheet walking on the pebbled floor with hurried but careful steps. I wondered who she was, because I was now convinced that it was a female of some status because the sheet was of silk and expensive, unlike the ones used by the village women. The lights were dim because the gas had burnt all night and was finishing. There was no one in the street and even the stray dogs were missing. I decided to follow this unusual figure who was in such a hurry, turning frequently to check if she was seen.

She left the village and at the outskirts she suddenly turned and started climbing the steps leading to the temple which my great grandfather, Daulat Singh, had built for Radha, Krishna and Hanumanji. I was surprised to see someone visiting the temple at this time, when the temple was closed because the pujari had died two weeks ago. I was too sick to appoint a new pujari, but was also against appointing Pandit Baldev Sharma's young grandson, Rattan Lal. Pandit Baldev Sharma was our family priest and served us for over forty years. He was a real Brahmin and a devotee of Lord Krishna and Hanuman. His family served ours from one generation to the next, but his grandson is not a good man. I did not like him and I wanted his son to return from Varanasi and settle down in the temple premises.

The entire place was bathed in the silvery light cast by the full moon but seemed to be empty. Even the monkeys, who are a known menace for the devotees, were not there. The figure started climbing the steps to the main temple and reached the veranda in front of the closed iron door. She bent down to pay her respects to the deities inside the temple and then turned left.

I followed and saw her waiting in front of the wooden door to the room meant for the pujari. The door opened and I saw a young man wearing a dhoti come out holding a torch. He flashed the light all around. After convincing himself, he opened the door wide and they both went inside. The door closed. It was all done so quickly that I couldn't enter and the room was sealed, so no fresh air could enter. I went around and found a small window at a higher level. It was open and I entered and took my place on it.

It was dark and I found that the gas lantern was lit, but half the room was still in darkness. I waited, concentrating on the conversation and trying to recognize the figures. Suddenly the room was bright enough for me to see the figure with the white sheet. I couldn't believe my eyes. It was my daughter, Rani, clad in a red sari with heavy jewellery. She looked somewhat nervous but not scared. It seemed she had come on her own. The figure turned after placing the lantern at a higher level, Oh my God! It was Rattan Lal, Baldev Sharma's grandson.

He was young, not even in his early twenties, tall, well built, with sharp features, a fair complexion and a muscular body. But his eyes had a lusty, treacherous glint. I looked at Rani, so innocent, heading for some trouble, but being defenceless I waited. She started talking while taking a seat on the floor next to the man who had by then seated himself on a cushion facing her. He held both her hands and started talking slowly, almost in a whisper and it was difficult for me to hear. So I came down and sat next to them on the bed.

He was holding her hands and urging her to talk. She started telling him her past.

***

Rani's Story

My mother died when I was twelve. My father was not interested in a second marriage but my grandmother, Sumitra Devi, was too strong for my father, who earlier even blamed her for my mother's death. My grandmother never liked my mother, because she was known to be good, kind, beautiful and with a pleasing personality by people inside and beyond the village.

My mother was innocent and very scared of her mother-in-law. My grandmother tortured her regularly, while my grandfather, Chaudhary Devi Singh, was alive, because she doubted the intentions of her own husband, owing to her beauty. My father loved her dearly until his mother turned him against her and almost made him doubt her character.

My grandfather died suddenly. My grandmother started talking to my father about my mother's bad character but the latter did not listen. This alarmed my mother so she forced my father to get me married early. In a hurry, they found the only son of Zamindar Himmat Singh of Doli, Amroha and without making adequate inquiries, I was wedded to him. I was young, not yet eleven, so I stayed in my father's home till I was thirteen. When I reached puberty there was gauna and I was sent to my in-laws' house.

It was a big zamindari earlier but even when I entered, after the abolition of zamindari, though it had lost its very rich status, it was still good, and they believed in lavish living. My father-in-law was very fond of music, dance, wine and rich food. Their only son, who was just sixteen, had the same habits. He was not fully educated and father and son frequently went out together. One day, my husband who never had sex with me asked for my jewellery. I refused and since he was drunk he gave me a good beating.

I returned home. My father now had a second wife after my mother died. She had a one-year-old son. My stepmother was my grandmother's niece, Sumitra, and was over thirty, ugly and with rough manners. There was no love between husband and wife and I found my father very lonely and drunk most of the time. I had come to stay but my stepmother's behaviour forced me to leave. I was not happy and now the rumour has spread that I am barren and my husband who has never had sex with me joined his parents in spreading the story.

My friend Mira told me to come here and see you because she had a son after your treatment in Sirsa, so I came. You have performed a great favour to Mira, Ram Kumar Bhardwaj's granddaughter, who was married in Sirsa. She is so grateful to you.

***

I saw my daughter crying, almost losing herself. The man got up and brought a glass of water. I saw him put some white powder into it. I did not want Rani to drink but in my helplessness I couldn't.

'Mira told me to visit you in my wedding dress.' The man nodded, replied that she would conceive after a few more visits to his house and that she should come at around the same time. Then he rose and brought out the sacred Bhagavad Gita and a small bamboo broom. He asked her to close her eyes and started chanting mantras touching Rani's head with the broom periodically.

I saw Rani swaying her head from side to side and then place it on his lap as though not fully conscious. He waited for some time, continuing to stroke her head gently. He then picked her up and put her on the bed and started stripping her.

I couldn't watch my own daughter almost stark naked so I turned my face. However, I wished to ensure he was would not kill her. So after a while I turned. I saw him naked on my daughter. The scene made me sick but I was helpless. I thought, 'I am a mere soul, I can't do anything.' I waited and then all was quiet.

It was dawn, when a knock on the door awakened them and he hurriedly left the bed. He covered Rani and went to the other room. He returned after some time fully bathed and in a fresh saffron dhoti, his forehead smeared with a sandalwood tika. He jerked Rani roughly to awaken her, and then holding her hair pulled her up. She opened her eyes, looked around and then looking at herself jumped up and tried to cover herself with her sari. She was in tears as she got dressed while this dirty young priest continued looking at her with a malicious smile. She got dressed and bent down to touch his feet while crying. He bent down to bless her and after that tried to hold her in his arms for a while. She tried to struggle but he only laughed.

There was another knock on the door and as he released her, he whispered, 'Get out but I promise, like Mira, you will also have a son.'

She removed her two kangans and gave them to him. They belonged to my wife, Sudha. I felt sad for my daughter, rather ashamed, but then argued that she had nowhere to go. My son-in-law was under the control of his mother, my second wife has a doubtful character and Ramia, Rani's husband is impotent – a man who has no urge for sex with his wife. However there must be a child to satisfy the in-laws. If she is successful all will be well, as her husband will not dare to utter a word because of his defect. This almost made me satisfied.

I saw Rani enter the side room. The pandit opened his cupboard and brought out a small tin box. He unlocked it and I saw some very expensive jewellery inside. My wife's kangans were also put inside. I was sad but there were no tears. The soul doesn't cry. The door was opened and the man outside remarked, 'It is late.'

'Yes,' he said and gave the keys to the local person working as the servant of the temple. The temple doors were opened and the bells started tolling.

Ramia, I followed Rani and she entered the haveli without being seen by anyone. Then I returned to the temple. I looked at the deity for the first time after many years. You know I was an atheist, but with my head bent down, I prayed. I accepted that there is someone above all of us, even when the caretakers of God's house are filthy and corrupt. People started entering and for the first time I admired their faith. I decided to watch the activities of this priest whom I had rejected before getting sick, and placed myself on the temple parapet.

The priest is young, handsome and has a good body. He is a smooth talker, particularly with women, and there is an aura of religious sanctity about him. The temple was closed at 11 a.m. and I followed the priest to his small kitchen where Tulsi, the wife of a farmer, was cooking his food.

He ate his food without talking to her. Perhaps he was being cautious or she may have been too old for his pleasure. He left the room sat under the pipal tree and went to sleep. He slept for almost half an hour, when Ram Dass approached to tell him that it is time for the recitation of the Bhagavad Gita and everyone was waiting.

The priest leapt up and holding the book which was lying

under the pillow followed Ram Dass. I trailed them as I now wanted to know all about him. He entered the haveli. The hall was filled with women sitting facing my photograph on the pedestal with a burning diya of pure ghee and incense sticks. The aroma was beautiful and for the first time, forgetting the incident of the night, I wanted to hear the recitation of the Bhagavad Gita. My soul is not fully developed, and so I cannot separate myself from my physical form as yet. And though I convinced myself that after my death nothing belonged to me, it is difficult Ramia, more so when I saw my photograph. I remember it was taken in Nainital when I was newly married to Sudha. She was a good wife.

The pandit took his seat by my photograph, and after offering flowers touched the sacred book to his forehead, closed his eyes for a second, recited more mantras and sprinkled Ganga water all around him. What pretence! He opened the book and started reading the first chapter of the Bhagavad Gita. I sat on the windowsill and looked around for Rani. She was not there. Most of the women were without purdha because of the belief that the man was too pure to cast lusty eyes on them. What a belief!

However, after listening to the chapter and accepting the power of Lord Krishna, I changed my mind and decided not to attach myself to family affairs, because I was no longer alive for them. When the recitation started, I listened carefully. I admired the way the man read the text, explained it, recited Sanskrit slokas and translated them into Hindi. He knew how to please women well, with his knowledge, sweet voice, the singing of slokas and so on.

I listened to the whole chapter, and as the gathering bowed to the priest and left, I left the zenana and went to the mardana. However there were very few people sitting on the floor with my son, and they were busy talking more about business than about me. What a world! One day you're a beloved son, husband and the head of your family, and your illness or injury makes the members agitated. However, death separates you. The body, that was once loved, was not liked by even my own family, and the aim was to cremate it as soon as possible.

The age-old rituals of death are performed and then every person's routine work—wife's, sister's, mother's, son's and daughter's is resumed. It was the same with my son. The newly rich man, just in his twenties, was busy discussing business. I laughed. I wanted to stay, but I remembered my mission to learn more about the priest, so I left for the temple. When I arrived there I saw him entering the same room. I went around and took my place at the window.

The room was bathed in sunlight but it was cool. This was because of the high ceiling. I looked down and what I saw almost made me jump. The ghori who tried to capture my skull was sitting on the floor. There was a coal fire in a small container in front of him, and he was heating some red oil on it. Then he brought out a bottle containing local alcohol and three pieces of meat. It was not past 5 p.m. The priest took a seat next to him and they started talking.

'Did you get the skull of the zamindar?'

'No.'

'Why?'

'Some people came and almost captured me. They also gave me a beating.' He exposed his body by raising his black dhoti.

'So, what happened?'

'I stayed for a while and then hid in the grove so that no one could see me.'

'So?'

'The bones were collected at night instead of in the morning and with that they also broke the skull into pieces.'

'That is bad.'

'I know.'

'So, what should we do now? You told me you would increase my sexual powers a hundred times over, once you got the skull and captured the soul of the zamindar.'

'I know but I was helpless.'

There was silence and they started drinking the alcohol. I looked at the red oil. To my utter surprise the large pieces of meat were placed on the coal and as they roasted, the red oil, that looked like blood was poured on it. Then the half-cooked meat was placed on two plates and both men started eating. However I found that the young priest was eating under compulsion.

They finished the meat and as the ghori rose he told the priest that he would get the skull but for the ritual, the priest would have to visit his place – a cremation ground near the river some distance from Baragaun. The priest nodded and touched his feet to get his blessings. The door was opened; the priest looked around and signalled to him to leave.

The priest returned, but as he was drunk, he got into bed without clearing the empty bottle and the burning coal. Soon he started snoring and I waited because I wanted to learn more.

It was getting dark when the man awakened, changed his dhoti and went out. The temple bells started tolling and the night prayer started but there were not many people. It was a short prayer and as he was about to close the temple door, I heard a woman calling him. He turned and said, 'Oh you have come, Mira!'

The woman took out a bundle of notes and gave it to him. She then told him in a sharp voice never to come to her home again. He laughed and told her that the bundle was too small in lieu of the son he gave her, so she had better come with all her jewellery or he would inform her husband. The woman paled and turned away.

It was dark and the single lantern in front of the temple door cast its light on the woman who appeared helpless. The priest laughed and turned to his room, telling her to get out and bring the jewellery. The woman waited for a while, and then left. I took my seat again and watched the man. He locked the door, took out a bottle and started drinking after putting the money in the cupboard. It was a starry night and a cool breeze was blowing. I started feeling tired but every day I was gaining strength and energy.

There was a knock at midnight. The priest, who was drunk, rose struggling to the door and after asking who it was, opened it. To my utter surprise it was Mira covered from head to toe in a white sheet. He looked at her, smiled and asked whether she had brought the jewellery. She nodded and came very close. He was about to hold her in his arms, and she too came close to him but when he held her, there was a cry and the man fell back, holding his stomach from where blood was pouring.

She picked up the bottle lying next to the bed and started beating his head. She bent down to confirm that he was dead. She took the key from under his pillow, opened the box in the cupboard, and took out select pieces of jewellery. She saw Rani's heavy gold bangles and she put them in her pocket. She then emptied the rest of the gold and money over his body and picking up the knife she hurriedly left the room.

The Third Day

IT WAS EXTREMELY hot and humid. The sky was overcast and there were hopes for the first rains of the season to start. This elated Ramia and he planned to sow some wheat. Leela also yielded a good quantity of milk every morning and the couple enjoyed kheer (milk pudding) in the evenings. Chunia rebuked her daughter-in-law and threatened to throw her out of the house if she ever tried to steal milk again.

It was midnight but since Ramia had no watch, he couldn't be sure. He waited outside as promised, in spite of the mosquito bites and humidity. A sudden breeze alarmed him because there was a saying that winds blow away clouds. However he heard his name called out and felt happy.

'I was waiting for you,' Ramia said.

'I had a good adventure and one secret of the haveli has made me excited to get to know more, so sit down and listen to me and don't talk because I have very little time to spend with you.'

'First tell me about the priest.'

There was a soft laugh and then a whisper, 'I will! Ramia, you being a Dalit, are treated as an untouchable, like an animal, without asking questions but now I am glad you have some incentive to learn more.'

'You're right because being a Dalit I was kept within the confines of village affairs. My life lay between my house and your haveli, but now I think I shall insist on my rights.'

***

Chaudhary Mohan Singh Visits Mira's House

When I left you before dawn, today, I just about reached the village pond when to the left, along Bhardwaj Street, named after the freedom fighter Ram Kumar Bhardwaj, I heard a woman weeping inside a house. I couldn't control myself and went in. The house was locked but I could hear the sound of sobbing. I looked around, but there was no vent for me to enter. I went around the house, and then at the courtyard I found a vent at a higher level, just large enough for me to enter.

To my surprise I found Mira, the woman who had stabbed the priest, holding her son who was in deep sleep, crying. As I watched, the door opened and a woman entered with a tray of food. She increased the gas burning in the lantern and the flame flooded the entire room. It was not Bimla Bhabhi, the wife of the freedom fighter, Ram Kumar Bhardwaj, who was elected as the member of the legislature three times, but was shot dead at Lucknow.

I remember how his death made village Mauli the den of the VIPs of the ruling Congress Party. At that time, his house was more important than the haveli and they named the street after him. They also elected Bimla, his wife, as the leader of the panchayat of five villages and plenty of money was given to rehabilitate the family.

The woman who entered Mira's room was Kamala, the wife of their son, Kirpa Ram Bhardwaj. She sat next to the girl and whispered, 'Don't cry and forget everything, even about the body which the police can't seem to find.'

'What happened to it?'

'I don't know and nor do the police. They think the man left the temple complex on his own. They do not think he is dead.'

She placed some food in the plate and urged the girl to eat. Then suddenly she saw a pair of bangles lying next to the pillow. The woman picked them up and asked, 'from where did you get these bangles?'

'From the priest's house, but why are you interested?'

'I am interested,' the woman replied, 'because they belong to Dhai Ma and except for me, my mother-in-law and Sudha no one knows about these bangles. They are very expensive because of the stones.'

'Who is Dhai Ma?'

'It is an old secret of the haveli, which even the zamindar who died three days ago was not aware of.'

The girl forgot everything, and wiping her tears took a comfortable seat next to her mother to listen to her. The voices were too low for me to hear, so I changed my position to sit closer to them. And this is what Kamala narrated:

***

Kamala Bhardwaj Talks about Dhai Ma's Secret

The haveli was not as palatial earlier, and the new wing with the good furnishing and expensive set-up was built when Chaudhary Zoravar Singh died in December 1932. After the death of Suman, his first wife, whose son was Devi Singh, he had taken on two other wives – Savitri Devi and Sumitra – who survived him. Chaudhary Devi Singh was the only son and was eighteen years old at the time, but was spoilt and acted like the son of a rich man enjoying life with women, wine and gambling.

His second mother, Savitri Devi, was a religious, pious woman, and though she ran the zenana with an iron hand, she had no control over the spoilt son, more so after the death of her husband, a kind, honest, religious man, who believed in simple living. He did keep the English rulers happy by giving more lagan and expensive gifts, but he never entertained them in the haveli.

It was said that he bathed in the waters of the Ganga before consuming any food after visiting the offices of the English. He had sixteen villages and some remained with him but he was not given the title of talukdar. Chaudhary Zoravar Singh changed and started visiting kothas and brought nautch girls into the haveli. When his wife died, he married Savitri Devi, a maid, and then young Sumitra, a nautch girl.

Chaudhary Devi Singh wanted more villages and a title, so he decided to please the English rulers more, by entertaining them in the haveli, for which he expanded the section of the mardana (the men's wing) with a new building that had a palatial hall, a dance floor for the nautch girls, bedrooms and a special kitchen to cook non-vegetarian food, which was never served inside the haveli. However, he maintained the zenana wing as it was. The surroundings and the river bank next to the haveli were beautified for fishing, and the zamindar's neglected forests were made suitable for hunting.

All these changes kept the new zamindar busy for a few months, but money came in from more lagan from the villages. The locals complained but there was no relief for them. My father-in-law, Ram Kumar Bhardwaj, was a freedom fighter and he was in and out of prison too frequently to be able to look after the locals. During that time our house was in a shambles owing to a lack of money. But Savitri Devi continued helping my mother-in-law and even sent my future husband, Kirpa Ram, who was only five at that time, to Kashi for studies. Life was very hard for my mother-in-law but all was well with help from the haveli and occasionally, even my father-in-law took refuge in the temple complex till he was sent to the Andaman Islands, called Kala Pani by the British. He spent ten years in a cell there, but survived.

He returned home ill with tuberculosis. There was no treatment for it at that time. However, our local vaid cured him. And in 1940, he was honoured by Gandhiji, who visited this house for his cremation.

The new zamindar and the people of Mauli, even though they didn't take part in the fight for the freedom, always respected the Bhardwaj family and the zamindarin continued helping the wife and young son. In order to get some help for her spoilt son and to keep him under control the zamindarin looked for a suitable girl and found Dhani Devi.

She was the only daughter of the zamindar of Kashipur. Though not very beautiful, she was tall, had a good figure, was very interested in music and dance, and even excelled in horse riding. However she was very bold, and the senior zamindarin, Savitri Devi, started disliking her. My mother-in-law told me that Dhani Devi knew Savitri Devi's background. Actually the latter was from a good family but after the death of her parents, Chaudhary Bhola Singh brought her to the haveli as a young child. She was good looking and she grew up among the women of the zenana. She started falling in love with young Chaudhary Zoravar Singh, but resented his first marriage to Suman; otherwise she had a good character.

There was not much communication, as I was told, between the newlywed husband and wife Chaudhary Devi Singh and Dhani Devi, after the first night, and then the notorious events in the haveli started, for which Savitri Devi always blamed Dhani Devi. The entertainment in the new wing with music and dance by the nautch girls of Lucknow were frequent, and became part of the haveli. There was a rumour that the zamindar even provided girls along with alcohol to his guests, but all this was kept secret by the locals who were very scared of Chaudhary Devi Singh.

The young zamindar was not only tall, muscular and handsome, but a good horseman, yet he didn't allow Dhani Devi to ever come out of the haveli. After two years, there was a commotion in the haveli and in spite of trying to keep it secret it spread far and wide that the young zamindarin had left the haveli. The news reached Kashipur, and her parents blamed Devi Singh's family. Savitri Devi tried to arrange a second marriage for Devi Singh, but the zamindar was so disliked by the other respected families of North India that it was difficult.

Then the young zamindar started spending his days in

Sitapur. There was a rumour that he had fallen in love with the daughter of a natchnewali of Sitapur. This was when my mother-in-law started visiting the haveli and tried to force the senior zamindarin to get Devi Singh married, because he was now in Lucknow and had informed her regarding his forthcoming marriage to a girl called Deva Bai.

However nothing happened and one day Chaudhary Devi Singh brought his second wife with great pomp and show to the haveli and before his mother could object, carried his bride to the new wing of the mardana. For days there was no entertainment and at night the locals heard a melodious voice and also the sound of anklets and dancing. Some even saw two riders at dawn riding on the banks of the river. But no one saw the new zamindarin except her own servant, a man called Ramu, who became her trusted servant in the mardana. She never came out in front of the women or visited the zenana according to the orders of her mother-in-law, Savitri Devi.

Things continued in this manner, and with the passage of time, the zamindar's visits outside the village and the entertainment and presence of other women in the mardana almost stopped. He stopped taking an interest even in money matters and everything was controlled by Deva Bai with the help of Ramu. Savitri Devi resented this, and though Deva Bai never interfered in Savitri Devi's affairs, she became Savitri Devi's arch enemy. Then there was a rumour of a pregnancy and when the midwife Prulia, confirmed this even without seeing the face of the woman in purdha, there was a rumour that she was pregnant before marriage. This news spread far and wide and she was accused of having a loose character.

The baby was born in Lucknow and she returned when he was two months old. The welcome was not for her, but for the boy, who Savitri Devi took under her charge. Deva Bai was not allowed to see her child, but she kept quiet. This increased Chaudhary Devi Singh's admiration for his wife and he lost all interest in women, wine and gambling and almost became her slave. Savitri Devi continued looking after the child but at the age of five he was sent to Lucknow to the special school meant for zamindars and talukdars. The boy came during his holidays but loved only his father and grandmother.

His mind was poisoned against his mother by the ladies of the zenana. He only knew that after his birth, his mother who had a good character and belonged to a rich zamindar family of Kashipur died because of the indulgences of his father with Deva Bai. Time passed, but no one ever saw the new zamindarin in the open – not even the local women. The only servant who was close to her was Ramu but he never talked about his mistress.

As the child grew into a boy and the mother watched him being spoilt by his grandmother, she tried to interfere through her husband, but Savitri Devi, though old, was too strong to be stopped and the fear of the exposure of Deva Bai's origin prevented the zamindar from disturbing the routine of the house. Suddenly, money, property and jewellery came from Kashipur in Deva Bai's name. This alarmed the zamindar but he was too much in love with her to say anything, and kept his silence.

However Savitri Devi told every local woman that it must be the ill-gotten money from her mother from Sitapur. Many asked Ramu but there was complete silence. Then the zamindarin started her charity work. She built a school for girls, a temple complex, donated money to poor farmers for their daughters' weddings and opened a small dispensary.

All transactions were through Ramu but the credit went to the zamindar because the charities were always in his name. The local women decided to unite and form a committee. They went to the haveli to ask Deva Bai to become their chief, but she refused, and through Ramu, gave money to build a hall and to buy sewing machines for them to start village handicrafts for the poor, the unemployed, widows and others. A section of the locals started loving the woman and called her Dhai Ma and the time came when she became the Dhai Ma of village Mauli.

However, the son, Chaudhary Mohan Singh, who gave up his studies in the middle came home and started working against his mother by calling her a black-blooded woman who took his mother's life.

'They say you work for the needy and they worship you but the locals of the village do not worship you at all,' he said.

No one dared to speak and tell the truth. All over the village, there was great fear of Savitri Devi, more so because Chaudhary Devi Singh was not in good health and was paralysed on his left.

The boy, not yet seventeen, became the talk of the village. It was my mother-in-law and her son Kirpa Ram Bhardwaj, who had the courage to persuade the zamindar to make him settle down. There was great respect between Chaudhary Devi Singh and my future husband throughout. Chaudhary Devi Singh had greater respect for Savitri Devi than for Sumitra so he asked her to get the boy to settle down.

Sudha was the only daughter of Shri Narayan Singh, who was the Dewan of Rampur. Sudha and I were close friends, since my father, who was a silk merchant, lived in the same state ruled by the Nawab. Kirpa Ram was sent to arrange the marriage. It was done, and in their house he saw me and asked for my hand. Everything was arranged, and he returned home.

This was in December 1956 and the young heir to the zamindari refused to marry unless all the ceremonies and rituals were carried out only by his grandmother and father. He wanted to confirm that the other woman would not enter, at any stage during the marriage celebrations. This hurt Chaudhary Devi Singh and he decided not to attend the marriage. But by the next morning Savitri Devi told my mother-in-law that all was agreed because Deva Bai herself told her husband that she would not attend and that freed her husband to do so.

It was past 8 p.m. at night when Ramu Kaka came to our house. He asked my mother-in-law to accompany him to the temple complex. Though she was scared, she followed him. He asked her to wait behind the huge statue of Hanumanji, and a tall figure completely covered with a white sheet came up to her and said, 'Don't be scared. You're the only one whom I can trust with my secrets, because you will never tell anyone. Let that be a pact in front of Hanumanji.'

My mother-in-law nodded. There was a light and to her surprise she saw Deva Bai or Dhani Devi now not so young, standing in front of her.

Deva Bai gave her three bangles and told her give it to her daughter-in-law but after scratching out the name Dhani Devi written in the corner of each bangle. My mother-in-law looked at her with her mouth open and was so shocked, she couldn't talk.

'I am leaving the village tomorrow for a few days but will be back after the celebrations. Give these to Sudha on your behalf and Savitri Devi will not even suspect, because no one knows about these bangles. They belonged to my dead mother; they are very heavy and costly and I am sure Sudha will love to wear them.'

My mother-in-law took the bangles but she was crying for the woman who was cast out, not by her family, but by her own son. Everything was settled and the boy was happy that Deva Bai left the haveli on the same night.

***

'So Dhai Ma was Dhani Devi! But then how did she become a nautch girl?' Mira asked.

'I am tired so let us rest and we will talk tomorrow because I had to attend the sarpanchs' meeting.'

Mira smiled, 'Yes you're a sarpanch now instead of a grandma.'

***

Chaudhary Mohan Singh Takes Over the Story from Kamala

The boy woke up and was crying. I left both of them but for the first time cursed myself that I, Chaudhary Mohan Singh, never suspected that the woman who was labelled a nautch girl was my mother.

I went to the new section of the mardana that was occupied by my parents. When my father died, all the rituals were carried out by me and I saw to it that his nautch girl never entered the old and main haveli. The very next morning after my father's death Dhai Ma left the haveli, leaving her room wide open. I saw Ramu give the keys of her room and to my grandmother. She was about to take them, but the hatred inside me was so great, I returned the keys to the man who was so close to her, and issued an order that that part of the house was never to be opened. I saw tears in his eyes, but he nodded and left.

Today, I wanted to see my mother's rooms, but I found everything locked. There was no vent through which to enter. I remembered Ramu and went to the servants' quarters. His room was empty and I knew he had left the haveli. I felt sad. I was still sitting on the wall of the haveli when I remembered the death of my grandmother, Savitri Devi. She was so old yet so active, and I loved her. I remembered how she frequently asked for forgiveness from Dhani Devi and I wondered: Why forgiveness when she was not so close to her! She had a long, tormented time before her death. Following her death, Sumitra took over the zenana. Everyone cried except Ramu, who was now one of my personal servants, and they cried more after Sudha's death. I tried to talk to Ramu, but he never replied and continued serving me even during my illness, even though the old bones were not fit. However, he left once Sneh took over.

At my death bed, I asked Ram Dass about Dhai Ma! The only words he uttered were: 'She is alive. She never took anything from the treasury as stated by your grandmother, Sumitra.'

***

'They say blood is thicker than water. I remember calling Rani and telling her to find Dhai Ma for me and discover the secret. Ramia tell me whether you have seen her or not.'

'No, once she left the village, she never returned. There was no further charity or any other progress. The locals cried periodically and many asked Ramu who stayed with you till Ram Dass took over, for her whereabouts, but he never uttered a word.'

'Ramia I must now go to hear more. I am interested in discovering how Deva Bai became Dhani Devi!'

'Sahib it must have been a shock for your father because he married her thinking she is a nautch girl!'

'Yes! However, my father wanted me to talk to her several times, but I found her too religious and right minded, and it remained casual conversations, because I hated her.'

The Fourth Day

'RAMIA, AFTER LEAVING you I entered Bhardwaj's house. The woman was making tea. Mira sat on the bed and Kamala started talking.'

***

KAMALA BHARDWAJ CONTINUES DHAI MA'S STORY

Dhai Ma returned after the celebrations in the haveli were over. She came at night and discreetly entered the haveli. She was worried about her husband, Chaudhary Devi Singh, who was by now very sick and unable to even talk. However the presence of Dhai Ma made him happy.

One night Ramu knocked on our door and asked Kirpa Ram to rush to the haveli because the young zamindar, Mohan Singh, would not allow Dhai Ma to have her husband treated by the vaid who came with her from Kashi. He went, but Chaudhary Mohan Singh refused and wanted the vaid from Mauli to continue his treatment. That was the first time my husband met Dhai Ma. He was very impressed with the woman who had not only dignity but was firm in fighting for her husband's treatment.

Dhai Ma talked from behind the purdha and Savitri Devi was allowed entry into the modern newly furnished section of the mardana for the first time, to see her son. He had never seen Savitri Devi looking nervous before, and he was surprised. It looked as though Dhai Ma's voice had some effect on her. She left the wing within seconds and this also surprised young Chaudhary Mohan Singh. He listened to the woman and then suddenly gave way and left the wing. The new vaid started treating the zamindar and within a short time there was improvement in his condition, but he couldn't regain his speech.

My mother-in-law told me, that following that episode, a change came over the haveli. Savitri Devi almost stopped interfering in the mardana section and even Sumitra's niece, Sneh left. Chaudhary Mohan Singh continued opposing the vaid. One day Savitri Devi called my mother-in-law and told her to find out about this woman in the haveli because somehow her voice, way of talking and the figure, even behind the purdha, resembled Dhani Devi.

My mother-in-law wished to know more but the old lady refused to talk further. Then she confided that she didn't want to open the old can of worms regarding Dhani Devi now, when her son was so ill and the heir still believed that his mother, Dhani Devi, was dead. My mother-in-law told Kirpa Ram that the woman was on the verge of a nervous breakdown, and was scared that her lie would be revealed to her grandson and the locals. That was perhaps the reason Sumitra Devi became more powerful.

I got married to Kirpa Ram Bhardwaj in a simple ceremony at Rampur three months after Sudha. Sudha did not return to Rampur at that time. When we met she told me about her grand mother-in-law, Sumitra, and how she had taken over all her heavy jewellery and even the expensive bangles given by my mother-in-law, which had been given by Dhani Devi.

She said that somehow she was unable to adjust to her, especially during the long visit of her niece Sneh. She dreaded receiving the same treatment as Dhani Devi. When I asked about Dhai Ma she was aware of her, but never had the courage to even look at the new wing. However no one in the zenana was permitted to talk about her; as though she were a black spot on the reputation of the zamindar, according to him and his mother.

However, through a whisper here and a whisper there, she heard a lot about the woman and why the people of Mauli forgot her origin and looked at her as the kind mother – Dhai Ma.

Knowing my relationship with Sudha, Sumitra was alerted, and the close relationship between my mother-in-law and Savitri Devi was not as close. Even the visits to the haveli were infrequent. It was sad that she refused to allow Sudha to come to our house for dinner and almost made her a prisoner in the haveli.

Chaudhary Mohan Singh now got interested in politics so he joined my husband and went to Lucknow more often. Sudha was pregnant. All was well till she was four months pregnant when there was a sudden deterioration in Chaudhary Devi Singh's condition, and within a few hours he died. There was a hue and cry in the haveli and Chaudhary Mohan Singh took over the body casting aside his mother, Dhai Ma, telling her, through Ramu, not to cast her shadow on the dead body.

That day I heard whispers among the women of the village and some insisted that the wife, Dhai Ma, should take part in the last rites. This alarmed Savitri Devi and with Chaudhary Mohan Singh's help she prevented Dhai Ma from entering the zenana. The zamindar's body was cremated and there was no movement in the new wing of the mardana. I am sure if Dhai Ma had insisted she could have taken over the haveli because most of the villagers loved her.

All went as planned till the ceremony on the thirteenth day was performed and the seat of Mauli was lawfully handed over to Chaudhary Mohan Singh. The next day Ramu entered the mardana and in front of all handed over the keys of the new wing to the new zamindar. There were more whispers and somehow the young master was nervous and uncomfortable and he never asked the man where the woman was. So I believe Dhai Ma left the wing at night.

'Did she?' the girl asked.

'No she stayed with us till dawn.'

***

Dhani Devi's Story

I was the only daughter of the talukdar of Kashipur who was not only a rich man with twenty villages, but had earned lots of money through the sugar factories he owned in Kashi and Sitapur. Being the only daughter, I was spoilt, very frank and believed in independence. I had a good education at home, could speak English, was trained in classical music and dance, and was a good horse rider. My father believed in entertaining the English rulers and had considerable influence and power in the government.

Then my brother was born. He was almost fifteen years junior to me. My parents, as you can expect, were more interested in him then in me. However, I loved my brother and we were a happy family that had no vices like wine, women, gambling. I received my religious character from my parents and knew the Bhagavad Gita by heart. The part I loved best is where Lord Krishna says that nobody should stay silent when someone is cruel; by doing that he or she is performing an injustice to the soul.

My marriage with Chaudhary Devi Singh was fixed. My parents spent an enormous amount of money, gave gold, silver, horses and elephants besides money. My father gave me a palatial bungalow in Kashi and put some money in my name, unknown to his son-in-law. Only I knew this. I fell for my husband when I first saw him. He was a tall, handsome, muscular man, a good horse rider and well versed in shooting. The wedding was held and I was taken to Mauli.

The haveli was not as palatial as the one in Kashipur and even the zenana was not up to its standard. However, I decided to change, but all went flat when on the first day,

Chaudhary Devi Singh entered my room drunk and unable to talk. I couldn't control myself. I locked him in the room and spent the entire night in another room. I was young, brought up in a good environment where no one drank or believed in nautch kotha. In the morning the Chaudhary wanted to teach me a lesson but I was also determined to fight.

Thus started the frequent entertainments, the arrival of women, the free flow of wine, and everything that a woman and wife resents. However I kept my silence, for which Savitri Devi started blaming me, but I had a habit of relaying the facts and this further annoyed my mother-in-law. I too put my foot down, and was ready to teach them all a good lesson, to improve the haveli as well as help the local villagers, who had no temple complex, dispensary or school.

The women had to work for a living and there was poor drainage because of which the whole river and forest were polluted. But it all seemed impossible. I stayed for three months but when the differences between us went too far, I decided to leave the haveli on a well-planned trip to Kashi without my parents' knowledge.

The person who was happiest was Savitri Devi but I wanted her to mend her ways by telling her one night that if she uttered a word against me, I would reveal everything about her – her entry into the house and what happened while she ruled the zenana of Mauli. I knew she was a maid and had relations with her father-in-law. This also constrained my other mother-in-law, a nautch girl, who was the number two zamindarin, not to encourage her young niece to enter the mardana of the haveli and I stayed indoors and kept quiet.

When I entered the house overlooking the sacred Ganga at Kashi, I found that it was beautiful, palatial, superfly furnished and there were three servants with their families. One of them was Ramu and I started trusting him. He was a eunuch and periodically, dressed as a woman, he would go to Mauli, to get information for me. I started practising music and dance and Ramu found a kotha, where he placed his sister as a nautch girl. Her name was Kalyani; she found girls from good homes and taught them dancing.

Ramu, dressed as a nautch girl, invited Chaudhary Devi Singh to visit Kalyani's kotha in Sitapur. When the zamindar came, I, as Dhavi Bai, entertained him with my dance, music and wine. Occasionally, I found him looking at me closely, but then he fell in love with me. It was my chance.

We got married at Sitapur in the temple and the witnesses were my close friends Kalyani and Ramu. He wanted to take me to Mauli at once but I insisted on the construction of a new wing. It was done and furnished according to my desires under Ramu's guidance.

I now started planning. In Chaudhary Devi Singh I found a man who did not have the correct values of good character and kindness. He loved women, wine, nautch and music besides good living, and boasted that he always got whatever he wanted. This type of showing off constricted my heart and I was determined to take my revenge.

Once he told me how I resembled Dhani Devi, but then laughed and looking at me continued. 'I crushed her within three months. She cried for help like a fish in the pond with no water but I enjoyed myself and she left the haveli to die somewhere.'

'My mother, Savitri Devi, told me how proud she was of her rich parents, but she left for good.'

'Do you love your mother Sumitra Devi or Savitri Devi?' I asked. A red hue covered his face but he didn't reply.

He continued, 'I waited but there was no sign of her being alive and it was confirmed when her parents came to inquire. But they couldn't lawfully blame me.'

I delayed my return to Mauli repeatedly, till I was pregnant and then was ready to live in the new wing of the haveli as the new zamindarin. He agreed to everything, but I knew he was a cunning man, and I was prepared for anything because this was my only chance to take revenge.

I reached Mauli behind my purdha. I saw the crowd and the gathering of women outside the haveli. He carried me – Dhavi Bai to the mardana, challenging his mother to stop him. However, she did not, and stood there like a silent spectator. I was placed in the well-furnished wing. The bedroom had a hall outside, and a raised floor for dancing. I gave him a sarcastic laugh and asked him who would be dancing here? Like a determined, victorious man, he placed me on the carpet and told me, 'You will dance till I sleep.' In plain words he told me, 'I have brought a kotha here, not a wife, so behave the way I want.'

It shocked me but I knew that animals do not change with love; they need a stick and human treachery. I smiled and to tell you the truth I started hating him from that day, from the inner core of my heart. The life of Dhavi Bai started as a slave in a golden cage, from where she was required to fulfil the needs of the arrogant zamindar.

He didn't ask about Ramu and the latter started serving me only. In spite of being in the first weeks of my pregnancy I sang, put on anklets and danced, served wine and most of the time made him so drunk that he only opened his eyes by midday. Ramu helped me to have a tunnel constructed from my bedroom to the zenana and gave me news of the zenana periodically. Actually Sumitra considered him to be my kept man and often talked about him and laughed openly with the other women to upset me. For her, a dancer cannot distinguish between the status of men.

Earlier, he had this one-sided love – his wine, music and dance, which almost intoxicated him, but then his mother warned him to stay in his senses and after some months, to remarry. By that time my pregnancy was advanced. Ramu told me that Chaudhary Sahib visited the zenana periodically, where his mother provided him with low-caste young girls. He was like an animal and to tell you the truth I now loathed him.

Whatever his weaknesses were, with the passage of time he began depending on me and I took advantage of him. I went with him to Lucknow for the delivery. I knew that I would have twins, but Prulia did not reveal this. Your great grandmother was given enough money to buy land, the reason why she declared it a difficult delivery and I was taken to Lucknow. There my father helped to hush everything through the doctors.

I had twins, both healthy and beautiful. Ramu took one to Kashipur to my parents, and the other, who was slightly under-weight, was taken from me by Chaudhary Sahib. Sumitra Devi spread the rumour the baby born to Dhavi Bai was stillborn, and another, one left by a woman at the health clinic, was adopted by the zamindar. She gave him his name, Mohan Singh, after the name of her beloved brother.

We returned to Mauli and on the first day, he handed the boy to Sumitra Devi. When I asked for the reason, he said, 'Blue blood must be cared for by blue blood.'

I lost my temper and told him his blood was not pure and was surprised that he raised his hand to hit me, but then stopped. This animal-like character alarmed me further and I told Ramu to complete the tunnel because I wanted to see my son occasionally.

To tell you the truth, I fed the baby my milk and played with him there the entire night while the zamindar was drunk and his mother intoxicated with opium. The child started growing up and I was not allowed to see or to attend any ceremony at the zenana. When I asked my husband, he laughed and told me not to worry or spoil my figure because I was not meant for babies and that his son needed strong, good care, which could only be given by a royal woman. This made me try to discover Sumitra Devi's secret and Ramu found out that she had been a nautch girl in Kasganj.

At times he was ashamed of marrying me and he blamed his youth, money and wine in front of the local people. Once he told Ram Dass, his personal assistant, that I was not the zamindarin in the real sense and that he regarded me as his keep. This further added fuel to the fire.

My son was now six, and to keep him away from my shadow he was sent to school at Lucknow. The school was meant for the rich. I was happy because my other son was also admitted by my parents to the same school. My brother was about to complete his schooling, but died in an accident before he could. Ramu told me that the school form was filled in by my husband, and the name of the mother was given as the late Dhani Devi. I decided to keep my silence. The boy was never once allowed to see me when he came to the haveli for his holidays.

Then one day Chaudhary Devi Singh had a stroke. The doctors came and though he improved, he was paralysed on his left side. He also lost his speech. He was now at my mercy, but I wanted to look after him as a wife, to let him know that even a tawaif can be a better wife than Sumitra Devi. Day in and day out he suffered but I never sang a song or danced or even gave him wine. He begged but I refused, and I discovered a way to cure him. A vaid came from Kashi. Though at first his mother interfered, I put my foot down and the vaid stayed. The vaid treated him and within two months Chaudhary Devi Singh gained strength. The treatment lasted five months and he could stand up, walk and talk. He was now a changed man.

During this period I started my work for the villagers. I came out of purdha. During my stay as Dhani Devi very few women of the zenana had seen me. So I changed my style, dress and hair, covered my face and came out of the haveli. It shocked Sumitra Devi. She reported this to the recovering zamindar, but he was helpless. I talked to the locals through Kirpa Ram. I opened a dispensary where the vaid from Kashi treated people, and I built a temple complex where Baldev Sharma became the priest.

The tolling of the morning bells awakened the locals, who bathed and came to the temple. They heard Sharmaji recite slokas, and went home calm and ready for hard work. I opened a school for children and got the village pond cleaned out. The women who were sitting at home got sewing machines to work and produce handicrafts. Then I got more money from my father and built a hall where mass weddings of girls could be performed, to reduce the burden of wedding expenses. I did all this through Kirpa Ram, and the villagers called me Dhai Ma. I was no longer Dhavi Bai.

I realized that the poor and the rich have the same blood. You work for them, give them money and they forget your past deeds. Sumitra tried very hard, after realizing that Savitri Devi was too weak, to lie to the women about my past but no one listened and she was helpless. At this stage even Kirpa Ram requested me to tell the people the truth but the time was not ripe, so I held my tongue and continued with my work.

My son left Lucknow and returned home. He was spoilt even more now by Sumitra Devi. However I continued with my work. Sumitra Devi arranged his marriage when he was sixteen. Even then my husband, the ailing zamindar, was ashamed to project me as his wife and the mother of his son. This made me lose all interest, sympathy and devotion to this family and village. I sent Ramu to Kashi to get my house ready because I wanted to leave this internal love for my son forever.

When I returned, my husband was sick and that night I changed my style. I wore my wedding dress and entered the room. The way he looked at me, I wondered whether it would kill him, but I was so sad and uncaring that I wished to shock him. He went pale, looked at me with and his mouth open and tried to speak. I smiled and nodded.

He opened his arms to welcome me and cried, but I was very determined and could not pardon him. I stood in front of him while he cried and turned away. Then he said that he knew before the marriage that I was his wife, but married me to punish me till I lived, and now he felt ashamed.

His mother, Sumitra Devi, and his son visited him regularly because he was ill. Every morning and evening he started asking for me and almost pushed his mother and son out of his room but I never entered to see him. His personal servant, Ram Dass, requested Ramu to persuade me. Ram Dass was a good man. He was sad at the deteriorating condition of his master's health. He repeatedly asked me and sent messages through Ramu requesting me to meet his master, but I refused.

One night I was called because his health was so bad they did not think he would survive. Yes he was dying. I went dressed as Dhani Devi. He looked at me, smiled and there were tears in his eyes. He begged me to pardon him, and even though by then I had a heart of steel, I forgave him for everything he had done. I touched his forehead and asked him to Chant Ram's name for comfort and an easy death. Death came after three days of struggle and by now the boy and grandmother had surrounded the body. My secret remained between the two of us and I knew it would be safe because the dead don't talk. Everyone knows how the family treated me, but I kept my silence and decided to wait for thirteen days.

Ram Dass told Ramu that the son and grandmother had decided to remove me from the wing and put me up in a room near the barn of the haveli at night, so that there may not be a hue and cry from the locals, who were so fond of me. I had plenty of money, jewellery and expensive antiques and clothes, so I got active. Ramu informed Kirpa Ram Bhardwaj and also brought me out through the tunnel. Within two days, without the family's knowledge, all my goods were cleared out and reached my house in Kashi. Kirpa Ram was given the keys and the staff there was told to get the house ready for me.

My son, his grandmother, and Sumitra's niece came at night. They knocked on the door and gently opened it. The wing had beautiful gas chandeliers but only one in the corner was burning. The new zamindar may have my blood, but was hesitant to go near the bed and shake me, a woman, from deep sleep. However, Sumitra, being old, had already seen the deaths of her husband and son, and roughly shook the figure lying fully covered from head to feet.

The firmness of the body and no movement surprised her and I saw signs of fear on her face. She asked the young Mohan Singh to increase the light. What they saw paled them. Ramu and I were just behind the wall looking on with a smile at everything through an unseen mirror in the room. The room was stripped of everything. There were no expensive decoration pieces or jewellery; only a five-rupee note for Sumitra Devi, as token money to inspect the room.

She opened the cupboards and they were all empty. The old woman sat on the bed and started crying but the boy insisted that she leave and told her the room would now be given to Sudha. This surprised both women, but neither said anything.

We left the haveli and came here to you, because I was sure that my son would never search your house. However I must wait for your Kirpa Ram to escort me.

***

'My mother-in-law wiped her tears and escorted Dhai Ma to a side room. She asked her to rest.' Kamala Bhardwaj concluded.

The Fifth Day

'RAMIA ARE YOU AWAKE? I am a little late coming, because I wanted to find out everything about my so-called grandmother, Sumitra Devi. It is sad that a woman even in her late fifties could tell such lies and act with such cruelty towards her own kith and kin, just to keep herself above others.

Mira's grandmother, Bimla Bhardwaj, who was the same age as Sumitra Devi, spoke to her bahu, Kamala. The old woman was lying on the bed sipping her tea. She looked older than my grandmother. When Mira entered the room they started talking about our family.'

***

Bimla Bhardwaj Discusses the Zamindars of Mauli

The zamindari of Mauli is not very old. It was given in 1858 to Chaudhary Daulat Singh, a landowner in Mauli, who helped the British and saved some of their lives during the rebellion of 1857, when the people of India took up a stand to gain freedom.

Only a minority of the rich and royal families supported the rebellion. Most of them, like the rajas of Gwalior and Baroda, and several others refused. On the contrary, they helped the British with money and men and provided them with security. Those who joined the rebellion were looted and tortured and many were hanged. This was when the

British rulers were looking for more faithful, affluent Indians to join their side. So they created landholdings in the form of villages and appointed the landowners as zamindars, talukdars and rajas.

Thus Chaudhary Gopal Singh, son of Daulat Singh, in his middle age, was made the zamindar of Mauli and given ten villages. The only work these zamindars were required to do was to collect lagan from the farmers and hand a part of it over to the British.

Chaudhary Gopal Singh was a God-fearing man and so was his wife, Shobha Devi. The old house was demolished and a new palatial haveli was constructed for the zamindar. It had a zenana and a mardana section. This was done so that a strict purdha system could be maintained in the feudal family. Both male and female locals were employed to serve, and were given poor salaries. Others were forced to grow crops so that the zamindar could pay a rich lagan.

As time passed, the zamindar became rich, haughty and developed the habit of living lavishly. Gradually he became fond of comfort, women and wine besides gambling. His wife, Shobha Devi, was a religious woman and never came out of the zenana or took part in the management of the haveli. It was a strange system. The zenana had a separate entrance, a courtyard with a stone stand holding a tulsi plant in the centre, where the women could pray. Rooms with covered verandas encircled the entire courtyard.

The rooms were spacious and had high ceilings and small windows near the ceilings for the circulation of air. The women's section was served by the village women on low pay and men were only allowed in for heavy work. However this could only be done with the permission of the master of the house, and if any male servant entered the zenana, all the women went behind purdha.

The master lived in the men's section. This section had a main hall that served as a sitting room. The seating system consisted of a fully carpeted floor with cushions. The hall was decorated with chandeliers and the ancestors' portraits in silver and gold frames hung on the walls. At that time the haveli did not have a hall for nautch girls and the master lived a simple and religious life.

A son was born when the master was nineteen, and he was named Bhola Singh. The members of the British Raj demanded money and gold, which had to be paid to keep them happy, plus the officers had to be entertained frequently. Village Mauli was small and the local people comprised farmers, banias, Rajputs, Brahmins and Dalits.

There were no roads, sanitary systems, schools or dispensaries. The feudal lords had no time to look after their people. Marriages were fixed between families of their own status. The lifespan of the average Indian was not more than forty years and it was even less for women, as they frequently died during childbirth, due to early pregnancies and lack of medical help.

Every village had a temple and the locals, though poor, were religious and believed in the age-old customs; they were honest and worshipped the feudal lords as they did their gods and goddesses.

***

Chaudhary Mohan Singh Describes Life in the Haveli

Ramia I will tell you about life in the haveli. The zamindar lineage started with Daulat Singh. It continued through Chaudhary Gopal Singh, his son Bhola Singh, whose wife was Shakuntala, called Kunti after marriage. Next came Zoraver Singh, Chaudhary Devi Singh, then me, Chaudhary Mohan Singh, and now the new zamindar is my son, Chaudhary Gujral Singh. This is from the period 1859 to 1970.

However, what happened inside the haveli! Anyone who heard the accounts would most likely lose his mind. The simple feudals became haughty, loved luxury, women, wine and gambling. And all the money for this came from the local people who worked day and night to pay the lagan even when there was famine or other disasters like floods or drought. The women inside the haveli had no work except to please their master when required, so they either spent their time in gossip, religious pursuits or intrigues against each other to satisfy their egos.

No wonder a haveli like ours witnessed murders, unwanted deaths, lesbian acts, female infanticide, child marriages and ill health owing to lack of proper medical treatment. The reason for this was that the men were concerned only with their own entertainment – nautch girls, molestation of young Dalit girls, and also the women of the village. All this was accepted by the locals, as there was no law by which anyone could ask for justice. Ramia, I must tell you the naked truth that I discovered on my fifth day as a soul.

Life was simple in the haveli on the mount, and the building was small till my great grandfather, Zoravar Singh, became the zamindar. I believe he was almost six feet tall, fair with sharp features and most of his face was covered by a huge moustache. The locals feared his large red eyes and loud demanding voice. He was strong and healthy and was known to be a good horse rider. He excelled in shooting, and could swim the river like a fish. He didn't like the way his parents lived, never wanted to study, but was not yet fond of women, wine and gambling. However, failing in his mission to become talukdar he changed.

And that was why his parents arranged his marriage to Suman, the eldest daughter of the zamindar of Gangapur. However, he believed that a wife was only meant to deliver an heir and for the occasional enjoyment of sex. His visits to the zenana were few and far between. He changed the setup of the mardana and added a dance hall and a kitchen where non-vegetarian food could be cooked, though it was never touched by the women.

Following the rebellion of 1857, the British showed a more lenient face to the public, and they ruled through these feudal lords. So the zamindar of the village was all-in-all in providing food, law and justice to the local people.

The Devadasi cult flourished in the temples of the South, including Orissa, Chennai, Madurai and Gujarat. However, this was not present in the North. The temples hired the wives or would-be wives of the Lord, like Lord Jaganathan in Puri, to please him with worldly comforts and entertainment. How can one believe that the deity of a temple can appreciate or have such human failings like lust, greed and anger?

These girls were mainly from the poorer classes, whereby parents would offer them to the temple in lieu of getting a male child in the family or to save them from the lust of the rich feudal lords. These girls were trained in music and dance and had to entertain devotees by becoming the wives of the Lord. Since the Lord is immortal, it was considered that these girls would never become widows. People would call them on auspicious occasions to perform various puja rituals. However this was merely one of the means for the Brahmins of the flourishing, rich temples, to have sex.

The British didn't like this practice and introduced a law against it. However, it was not applied forcefully. The rebellion of 1857 affected their autocratic ways of rule. They were scared of the rich and powerful Brahmin community. Devadasi was a strong religious belief amongst the masses of India, and they were scared of another mutiny, so they silently allowed the cult to continue.

Many devadasis, looking to their futures and aiming for more money left the temples and became nautch girls in the North, particularly in places like Lucknow, Sitapur, Kashi, Kanpur, Kasganj, which soon became the dens of nautch girls. These girls excelled in music and dance and developed a high standard of living, and they then started teaching etiquette to the heirs of rich houses. In Lucknow, the kothas of dancers became hubs to learn manners, for sex training and to learn how to live in high society. Wealthy parents sent their young sons to attend these 'schools' and learn more about sex before getting married. Further, childhood marriage was the norm.

Thus Chaudhary Zoravar Singh, when he was only twenty-two started attending Meera Bai's kotha in Kasganj. His trips and extended stays away from the village remained a secret till one day he brought a girl called Sumitra home to help Suman with her young baby, Chaudhary Devi Singh. She was not only young but very beautiful and had a melodious voice. She entered the zenana and like any lesser member of the family started looking after the baby.

No one suspected her relationship with the zamindar but when Suman got pregnant twice, and the babies were stillborn, it alarmed her. She started doubting this girl, particularly, when, within a year of Sumitra's arrival, her mother-in-law, Kunti Devi, died in her sleep. The vaid pronounced her dead and blamed her heart but Suman knew that Kunti Devi had no such problem.

Suman informed her father and told him her doubts regarding female infanticide, because the babies were buried before she regained consciousness. Suman's father Rao Varinder Singh was a very clever man and loved only his son more than he did Suman. He placed a spy, Sunani, as his grandson's maid in the zenana.

Sumitra discovered this and was very angry. She reported the matter to Chaudhary Zoravar Singh, who told her to remain silent. By now Sunani had discovered and informed Suman about Sumitra's relationship with her husband and that they met at night, after Suman's milk had been drugged.

This disturbed Suman and she asked Zoravar Singh to send Sumitra away. Since Zoravar Singh was scared of Rao Sahib he agreed and she was sent to the old haveli in village Kaurali. However the zamindar now started meeting her in the haveli without Suman's knowledge, so the latter was happy. Sunani again put a doubt in the zamindarin's head regarding the fact that only one male member was ever alive to continue this zamindari.

The secret was out when the midwife Rumia, your great grandmother, told Sunani her version. She took them to the room which was converted into a temporary labour room when required by the family. Here she and Sumitra Devi, with Chaudhary Zoravar Singh's full knowledge, buried her two daughters. For days Suman was lost in grief and began hating her husband who now lived outside Mauli more frequently.

One day she decided to trap her husband with Sunani's help. They went to the old haveli and caught Sumitra and the zamindar involved in open sex. Sunani forced Suman to return quietly and then informed her father, Rao Sahib. This was a wrong move. The parents threatened Zoravar Singh, demanding that he break his relationship with a woman who was the daughter of the known kothawali, Gulabo of Kasganj.

Her name was actually Meera Bai, but she entered the house as Sumitra Devi. She brought her cousin, Ram Dass, a handsome young man to the haveli. He lived in the mardana but occasionally met Sumitra Devi when she wanted to. No one suspected the brother and sister, and gradually the brother became the zamindar's personal servant.

When Zoravar Singh refused to obey Rao Sahib, there was a fight and Rao Sahib warned him to mend his ways. The wide rift between husband and wife brought Sumitra back to the haveli. Zoravar Singh asked his wife, Suman, to leave. The latter like her mother-in-law Kunti was found dead, but the zamindar regarded this as a result of her frustration and told the police that it was suicide.

Soon after the tervien, he married Savitri Devi, a maid, who worked in the haveli, asking the locals to look after his son who was only three. However, his affair with Sumitra became the talk of the village, and thus within a short time he openly married her. Now there were two zamindarins in the haveli – the senior Savitri Devi and junior Sumitra Devi.

The zamindar's latest wife, Sumitra Devi, was young and

beautiful, and in her early twenties. She not only started ruling the zenana but also the mardana, where she decided to live. She brought music, dance, nautch girls, wine and gambling for her husband. The locals watched but could do nothing, because Chaudhary Zoravar Singh changed his interests from outdoor activities to indoor lavish living with his young wife, entertaining the nautch girls of Lucknow and Kashi and most of the time drowning himself in alcohol.

The young Chaudhary Devi Singh now started learning the ways of life in the haveli. At the age of eleven he was found dead drunk and was picked up by a local person. Though Savitri Devi tried, she was helpless because Sumitra Devi was the zamindar's favourite and very powerful in the zenana.

To start with, there was a rumour that Sumitra Devi wanted to kill Chaudhary Devi Singh but was scared of her husband who loved him dearly and often warned her to look after him carefully. The threat was enough for Sumitra Devi who was too clever and had only one mission, which was to rule the haveli. The entertainment in the haveli at times brought British officers to village Mauli. Fishing in the rivers, hunting in his forest, the nautch girls and the wine and feasts brought Chaudhary Zoravar Singh the title of Rai Sahib. Now Chaudhary Zoravar Singh was Rai Sahib Zoravar Singh of Mauli and for that he was indebted to Sumitra Devi.

The number of villages increased from ten to sixteen. For this the zamindar became even more of a slave to his wife and she started interfering with the money and jewellery kept inside the locker hidden in the mardana section. The British noticed the deteriorating condition of the child and almost forced the zamindar to send him to the special school in Lucknow. Thus Chaudhary Devi Singh was sent to Lucknow. This made Sumitra happy and she almost threw Sunani out of the haveli. Now there was nobody to stand against her.

She was happy, but then a rumour spread in the village about Ram Dass as a result of which, the police entered the haveli to learn more about him. They accused him of killing his wife before coming to the haveli. Though he denied this and gave Gulabo as a witness, Sumitra Devi distanced herself from her brother. However, through the influence of the mighty zamindar, he was freed and became the zamindar's personal servant. Nonetheless, there was a doubt about the relationship between Sumitra Devi and Ram Dass in the minds of the people.

Sumitra Devi tried hard to have a baby and now besides taking part in the entertainment, she invited many tantrics into the zenana. However she was not successful and she had to accept the only heir, Chaudhary Devi Singh, as her own son. The boy stayed in school for hardly three years when he was expelled for going to nautch girls' houses – he was not yet fourteen. He returned home and joined his father and became very close to Sumitra Devi, who encouraged all his bad habits. Thus a rift was created by her between father and son.

One day she brought her niece, Sneh, who was of the same age as the young Devi Singh. She encouraged the young couple but the father put his foot down and told Sumitra Devi to ask Sneh to leave. It was a known fact that Chaudhary Zoravar Singh didn't want his son to marry like him into a family with a reputation of the kotha. This hurt Sumitra's ego and from then onwards, she started fighting and made life inside and outside the haveli, unbearable for the zamindar. However he was now middle aged and he wanted to mend his ways. He wished to have good relations with the locals and arrange the marriage of his son with one of the good zamindar families.

A girl called Dhani Devi was selected. She was the daughter of the zamindar of Kashipur. Till the end Sumitra continued to press for her niece, Sneh, to marry Chaudhary Devi Singh. By this time, Zoravar Singh wanted to regain the prestige of his feudal family by bringing home a bride from a good, upper caste family. This made her so angry, that for days she ignored the zamindar, but the latter was determined. All went well and the marriage ceremony was performed at Kashipur.

Dhani Devi was not even twelve, so she was not sent to her in-laws home and was made to wait till she was fourteen. During these years Zoraver Singh's health deteriorated. The gona was performed and the new bride entered the haveli. She had character and a determined mind, so she fought for her rights. She refused to hand over her jewellery and money, kept her palatial house in Kashi a secret, and charmed all the women of the zenana.

Through them she discovered her mothers-in-law, Savitri and Sumitra Devi's past. Savitri Devi, who was older than Sumitra Devi, was not very active. Savitri Devi was an orphan raised in the haveli by the late Chaudhary Bhola Singh but always resented having to stay with the servants. She was a tall, good looking, religious, young woman but had an eye for the young master Zoravar Singh till Sumitra entered the haveli. The young Zoravar Singh had an affair with her but never wished to marry her. However, after Suman's death he did, so that she would care for his only son. He respected her more than he did Sumitra, because she came from a good family. Sumitra Devi had only one mission: to become the sole ruler of the haveli through her niece, Sneh and the next heir.

Dhani Devi brought her own maidservant from Kashipur, but Sumitra Devi did not allow this, and at the end Dhani Devi was left alone to fight on all fronts – Chaudhary Devi Singh, who hated her because she refused to be with him till he stopped drinking and Sumitra Devi who wanted her niece to be the zamindarin.

The rift between Ram Dass and Sumitra came to the surface after the police inquiry, which they were forced to stop when he was poisoned and got ill. Though he recovered, he could only talk in sign language. He knew who gave him the poison so he became Sumitra Devi's arch enemy. He never visited the zenana again and remained with Chaudhary Devi Singh, fully armed to save him from this woman.

Ramia, when I heard this about Ram Dass, I felt sad for him. Could you imagine that his own sister would poison him?

The Sixth Day

'RAMIA WAKE up and listen to me. I was on my way to the temple after leaving you here at dawn. I saw a man come out from behind the haveli. He held something in his hand which was covered with a white sheet. Taking quick steps, he entered the street called Vaid's Street. I followed him. I saw him looking around furtively, careful and alert to ensure that no one followed him. He knocked at Vaid Hakum Chand Sharma's door. It was opened and under the gas lantern held by an old woman, I was surprised to see Ram Dass.'

***

CHAUDHARY MOHAN SINGH DISCOVERS THAT RAM DASS HAS A SECRET

As he entered I also made a quick dash inside. This was the first time I had been inside Vaid Hakum Chand's house. Even though he is so old, he is still considered the best doctor in the village. The house was built with bricks and cement and had a well-kept lawn. But we were at the rear of the house, where there was a barn.

The barn had two cows and a goat. Next to it was a small room with a thatched roof. The door was opened and the room was lit by the same lamp the old woman was holding. I wondered how such an affluent man, could live in such a room. I thought it could be another entrance to the main sitting room; it was not. The room had one cot on which the old man was now trying to sit up, while his wife adjusted the cushion behind him.

The room was bare, with only one old wooden cupboard on which were two steel plates and two to three glasses. The man covered himself with a tattered khadi sheet and asked Ram Dass to sit on the side of the bed, while his wife went out to make tea.

'You called me?' Ram Dass asked. To hear the man talking like a normal person surprised me.

'Yes!' The old man spoke, 'I am going to die a helpless man as my son and his wife have taken over my house, money and all my possessions. Earlier they gave us food regularly, but now even that is not as promised, because I refused to sign a will in their favour. I am determined not to, because there is no love lost between us.

'I called you to remind you to take your future bride Karina and my wife after my death, as you promised. These are the signed papers giving everything to my deaf and dumb young daughter you have promised to marry.'

Ram Dass took the papers and then holding the old man's hands, said, 'When you saved my life after my wife poisoned me I couldn't talk. However you gave me hope and gradually I regained my powers of speech and hearing. I decided to marry your daughter as a token of my gratitude.

Throughout the period I was deaf and dumb, my wife, Sumitra, taunted me and I had to eat humble pie. But when I regained my health, speech and hearing, I felt in seventh heaven. I watched Sumitra closely. She is almost in her sixties but so healthy and active.'

'Your wife!' the vaid said, spilling his tea with surprise!

'Listen carefully to the truth,' Ram Dass replied.

***

Ram Dass Tells His Story

I am from Puri in Orissa. I am the son of the chief priest of Lord Jaganathan's temple. Being the only son, I was trained to take over his sacred seat after his death or if by chance he was unable to carry out his duties. My parents gave me everything – a good religious education including tantric education and I learned music.

The Lord's temple was rich and full of devadasis. At the age of sixteen I became the music and dance teacher. I was tall, handsome and had a muscular body. The cult of devadasis was at its peak at the time and the pandits of the temple were very powerful – next only to the royalty. The selection of devadasis was in my father's hands. The girls were mainly low caste Dalits or daughters of devotees who came with a promise that on the birth of a son they would donate their daughter to the Lord to serve as his wife, a devadasi in the temple.

The girls were aged six onwards. They were enrolled as devadasis in the temple and given clothes, food, shelter and an education, besides being taught music and dance. These girls were taken in at a tender age to save them from molestations by the rich upper classes, but to tell you the truth they were not safe from the priests. These girls helped the senior devadasis till they attained puberty.

After the first menstrual period there was a celebration and the girl became the Lord's wife. She spent the first night after being sworn in, alone in a room specially reserved for piercing the nathni (breaking of the hymen). As a young boy I was not inquisitive, but soon discovered that this was done by the chief temple priest or a junior one, if the king of Puri or the prince refused. This shocked me because I thought these young women were sacred and the Lord's true wives.

I completed my education at Konark under the guardianship of the learned music and dance artist and singer, Pandit Raviji Maharaj and I joined the temple complex under my father. I was enrolled as the master in the department of music and dance of Jaganathan and had to teach young girls, between seven to eight years. They were happy in the temple because of the protection, shelter, food and education they got along with learning music and dance.

Here I met Sumitra whose name as a devadasi was Krima. She was from a fishing village on Chilika Lake. She was nine years old, uneducated, bold and beautiful. She was fair, had blue eyes, long black hair, and appeared to be the progeny of a feudal lord of the area, because the parents were dark and ugly. She was not only bold but grown up for her age. She had a beautiful voice and was talented in the art of dance and music. She also had the knack of making friends with everyone and was popular with the temple staff and senior devadasis.

In those days child marriage was part of Hindu Society because of the danger of girls being picked by the zamindars and to save them from molestation by declaring them as married women. So I was married to Seema, my guru's grand daughter in Konark. At six, Seema lived with her grandparents and we never met till after the marriage. When I completed my education and reached home at sixteen years of age, there was a gona. The celebrations lasted a week at Konark and I brought Seema, aged fourteen, home. She was young, good looking, delicate and had all the characteristics of a girl brought up in an orthodox pandit's family. She loved religious rituals and age-old customs and was overly superstitious.

However, she was uneducated and after the first year of passion, I started ignoring her even though she was the apple of my parents' eyes and they were very proud of her. I told my father that I wanted her to be educated and learn dance and music. But he rebuked me for thinking of her on a par with devadasis and holding such nasty thoughts about my wife.

I was not satisfied with Seema, but within two years I became the father of a son, Sidharath. I loved him and underwent all the rituals and promises of being a good husband in front of the Lord.

When the time came to break Krima's nethni, there was a celebration in the temple and I discovered that my father had performed the ceremony. I was not interested in these rituals but then something unusual happened. One day as I was teaching some dance steps, I found Krima was not paying attention. I tried my best to make her attentive, but to no avail. I lost my temper and almost slapped her. She went red and left the class. For days she didn't return. I was worried and then discovered that she was bleeding and had fever for a few days. This was soon after the initiation ceremony performed by my father and the vaid told her to rest.

When she rejoined my class she was very pale and had lost weight. I felt sorry and apologized for my behaviour when we were alone. She stood like a statue and tears streamed down her cheeks. Something made me go close to her and I almost hugged her. With that the closeness, attraction or love started along with my continuing frustration with Seema.

I was twenty and she was fourteen, and we soon became lovers. She could really attract men and please them with her melodious voice, entertaining conversation and sex. Besides, she was beautiful and had a good figure. We were often seen together but no one bothered in the temple. Even my father laughed, because these incidents were viewed lightly in the devadasi cult. The birth of a devadasi's child was considered 'Dharm Santan'. They were under oath never to expose the father's name.

Seema didn't care either. She was busy caring for our child, Sidhharth, and my parents to bother about me. Soon Seema and I were living together in the same house with no interest in each other. I gave Krima the name Sumitra and this became her name between us.

At this time, the temple was making money and the attraction of devadasis with their dance and music, besides their availability as women was at a peak. It brought not only local people, but even people from outside and the cult which was meant to entertain the Lord, now became nothing short of prostitution. Though people invited devadasis for rituals during weddings, they were now looked down upon as a source of money and sex. The British tried to stop this, but failed because the temple pandits and local royalty were very strong and the memory of the 1857 mutiny was fresh in their minds.

I now wanted to marry Sumitra, but when I mentioned this to my father he not only put his foot down he asked Krima to leave the temple complex. That night both of us left Puri. She wanted me to take my wife's money and jewellery, which I did and we arrived at Lucknow.

There we underwent a court marriage and were legally declared husband and wife. I, Ram Dass, the son of the chief priest of Jaganathan became an ordinary man in Lucknow with my pregnant wife, Sumitra. Sumitra could not adjust to the single room hired by me, more so after the birth of a baby girl we named Sneh. The money was almost used up, and this forced me to take up a job. However it was an ordinary teacher's salary and Sumitra was not happy. I frequently had the urge to return to my parents but couldn't because of the young mother and girl. With the passage of time, there were several fights but I still loved her and was proud of her beauty.

One day I returned early from the school and found the door locked. I waited and was worried. She returned with a middle-aged woman called Gulabo. She called her aunty and it seems she had been friendly with her for some time. To me, the woman appeared of low character, but I kept my silence.

One day she asked me if she could visit Gulabo's haveli. I didn't suspect anything and gave my permission. Now Sumitra was happy; but I was blind. My eyes opened when she asked me if she could go to Kasganj to Gulabo's parents' house for a few days. I agreed and she left with our daughter. When she did not return after one week, I decided to go to Kasganj.

I couldn't believe what I saw there. Gulabo had opened a kotha for music, dance and mujra in the evenings and Sumitra was the main singer and dancer. It angered me but she told me that she had taken up this profession and did not care whether I stayed or not. Sumitra, now as Meera Bai, was a very good actress. She was clever in gaining your favour either by talking or crying or attracting you with sex. To tell you the truth, I was a fool as I decided to stay.

Soon she became the star of Kasganj and I was not her husband but the masterji while Gulabo managed Meera Bai's kotha, because Sumitra as Meera Bai became famous. One day she met Chaudhary Zoravar Singh, the spoilt young zamindar of Mauli. By now she was twenty and he was in his late twenties, a married man with a son. He was rich and Meera Bai wanted money and protection for her daughter, now nine. The Chaudhary and Meera Bai hatched a plot between them and entered the zamindar's house. Sneh was left as her niece with Gulabo and I accompanied her as her cousin to Mauli. I discovered later at the haveli that Sneh was a eunuch.

I didn't like the establishment but still loved her and my daughter and she knew this. In her own way she also loved me but money was everything for her. I thought of the money, status and good life at Puri and decided to go there particularly to save my daughter from this profession. I visited the place under disguise.

What I saw made me realize I had no place in the family. My father was old, my mother had died and Seema was sedate, looking beautiful in a white sari. She was religious and devoted to Sidhharth who was now fifteen. He was my replica and was called Chhote Sahib – the heir to the highest seat of the temple of the Lord. I would have gone to my father and asked for pardon, but the men in the hotel who didn't know who I was, told me how the family suffered till they disowned the son and named the grandson the heir. My mother died following a heart attack, within a year. She would cry for her son but no one knew where I was. But my father found out about Sumitra becoming a nautch girl, through someone who visited Lucknow, and blamed me for running after such a girl.

I left Puri and joined Sumitra in the haveli. There I first stayed with her as her cousin but then became Chaudhary Zoravar Singh's personal companion. He never doubted our relationship. Her cruel behaviour towards Chaudhary Zoravar Singh's wife, killing her two girls at birth, and even Kunti Devi, his own mother, made me hate her and the final blow came when Suman was given poison in her milk and died in her sleep.

Thus Sumitra Devi became the zamindarin of a rich house. Now she wanted to get rid of me and when I warned her, she also drugged me through my own daughter, who innocently and unknowingly brought me milk.

Then Vaidji, you saved me and I decided to act deaf and dumb and watch my wife – the woman who took my future and left me on the road. I have now decided to leave Mauli and go to Puri. There I planned to live in disguise and serve the Lord. If you still wish it, I shall take your daughter, but last night I decided to get her married to someone in Puri.

I shall return to look after your daughter and your wife, whenever they require me. I have to be with my family and now hope my father will accept me as a family member. I wrote to Seema and the reply came yesterday. The house is big and there is money, I am confident Seema will accept your family as ours and we will soon find someone for your daughter.

***

Chaudhary Mohan Singh Takes Over the Narrative from Ram Dass

Ram Dass took out a letter and handed it to the vaid. Under the dim light he read the letter from Ram Dass' wife asking him to return soon, as Sidhharth was getting married and his father was ill and wanted to see him.

'What about Sneh?' the vaid asked.

'I am no longer interested in the mother and her daughter. They are both the same, but believe me they will suffer. Seema's murder and then making Sneh marry Chaudhary Mohan Singh after getting rid of Sudha was not good. I am sure God will take revenge.'

The Vaid's wife came close to Ram Dass and asked, 'Are you talking about Sudha?'

'Yes.'

'Where is she?'

'I don't know.'

'Then whose cremation was performed?' the Vaid's wife inquired.

'Gulabo's,' Ram Dass replied. 'She was too old and sick to stay alone at Kasganj and was brought here to live in the haveli where she died. That same morning, Sudha was drugged and was to be thrown into the river, but Sunani found out and informed Rao Sahib, who brought his men along and took her home.'

Ram Dass got up and asked Vaidji what he should do about the papers. The old man told him to keep them in safe custody till all was over. He said that Ram Dass must fight so that his wife and daughter got their rights. There were tears in the old man's eyes as he thought of his son's treachery. He blessed Ram Dass, who was only in his late fifties, but looked old and haggard. He marvelled at how a woman could make or break a man. He asked about Sudha.

'I shall tell you tomorrow,' Ram Dass said. 'As such I am here till the ceremony of the thirteenth day.'

However, when the same man walked towards the haveli he looked determined; someone with a mission. I followed him. He entered the zenana without a care, knocked at the door and when the woman who opened the door was about to speak, he shut her mouth with his hand and pushed her inside. I entered with him and saw that the room had everything which belonged to my wife, Sudha. Sumitra Devi looked at the man, stunned by his action and sat on the bed, but soon gained control and smiled.

She asked him why he had entered her room so forcefully. There was no reply till he took a key from under the pillow. The woman was now alarmed and started fighting but he hit her on the face and pushed her so hard that she fell to the ground. He opened the cupboard and took out a wooden box beautifully carved with gold and silver work. He placed it on the table and I knew it belonged to Sudha. He opened it, selected some jewellery and looking at the woman, started talking. Hearing the dumb man speak, Sumitra paled.

'I am going home and taking Seema's jewellery. I want you to leave the haveli or the police will arrest you. But before that, inform the zamindar that Sneh is not his mother because you and I know that our daughter is a eunuch, and though we raised her as a female she can't have a child. So before I leave on the thirteenth day ceremony, I want you and Sneh to leave this haveli on the same day.

'Where will we go?' Sumitra Devi asked.

'Go to Kasganj and stay in Gulabo's house with your daughter. She can carry on the same profession as yours.'

'Where are you going?' she asked.

'To Puri to live with my wife, Seema,' he said and laughed the sarcastic hollow laugh of a frustrated man. As he went towards the door, I saw the woman pick up something to hit his head. I touched him, he turned and the blow missed him. He closed the door, held the woman and firmly, and gave her a beating, leaving her almost half dead, and left the zenana.

The Seventh Day

'RAMIA COME OUT and sit with me, I have exciting news for you.'

Ramia got up and touched his forehead; it was still hot. He wondered at the cause of his headache. He took the small packet given by Vaid Kesi, the son of the old man, to be taken with water, gently opened the door and took his seat on the same stone platform.

'Aren't you well?' the voice asked.

'No.'

'Have you taken any medicine?'

'Yes, but the Vaid's son is not as good as the old man,' Ramia replied.

'I know.'

'He is very greedy he charged me, a poor Dalit, one rupee,

'How expensive! Sit down and relax.'

'I am fine now, please talk Sir!'

'Sudha is alive and my son, the heir to this estate is Sudha's son not Sneh's. I looked for Ram Dass expecting him to be at the Vaid's house but I could not see him. Finally I saw him. He no longer looked tired; on the contrary he looked rather young and fresh, with a youthful spring in his step. He entered the house and I followed. He gave the old woman a basket which had some fruit and food besides milk and gur (jaggery).

'How are things at the haveli?' the Vaid asked.

'All is well.'

'What about Sumitra and Sneh?'

'I took them to task and saw to it that they vacate before I leave.'

***

Ram Dass Continues His Narrative

Chaudhary Mohan Singh was married early because he was creating problems for the young girls of the village. He not only scared them with lion cubs and snakes, but physically hurt them and even molested a few Dalit girls of other villages.

Chaudhary Devi Singh was sick of complaints. He started looking for a girl. The other zamindars knew about the mysterious death of his mother and wife, and the rumour that the new zamindarin was a nautch girl. They were not in favour of an alliance with his son. This pleased Sumitra and she brought Sneh to the haveli.

At this stage my conscience pricked me and I fought with Sumitra, threatening to tell the zamindar. This angered the proud, rich zamindarin and she decided to get rid of me. First she tried to send me to Puri to meet my family and get more money, failing which she put poison in my milk. It was God's will that I didn't drink the milk because I had an upset stomach and gave it to the cat who drank it and died.

For days she kept a low profile because she knew I suspected her. I told her that if she ever tried to come in my way, I would disclose her past. This kept her quiet, but only with me. She continued to display her daughter whenever Chaudhary Mohan Singh was in the zenana.

You have seen Sneh. She was young and knew the art of attracting the opposite sex, as she was taught by Gulabo and Sumitra. Unfortunately she had a thick, hoarse voice and she was a eunuch, brought up as a female. Sumitra was confident that it would be all right, since the doctors in Lucknow had told her that she could get married, but would not be able to conceive.

Sumitra was keen on the marriage and decided that a child could be adopted without Chaudhary Mohan Singh's knowledge, since he was always under the influence of women, wine and nautch girls.

The Dewan Sahib of Rampur once visited the haveli and liked the boy. Sudha was the only daughter of Rao Ravinder Singh, the Dewan to the Nawab of Rampur. He had no child for several years, and adopted Soni Devi. But within a year Sudha was born. He was rich and she was the sole inheritor of her father's vast fortune and property.

Chaudhary Devi Singh fixed the alliance and without bothering about his zamindarin, Sumitra Devi, he went ahead with the marriage. The ceremony was celebrated with great pomp and show.

The new section of the haveli was vacated, which Sumitra resented, and furnished for the newlywed couple. The resentment between Sumitra and the Chaudhary increased to the extent that he refused to see her for days. However, even after Sudha's arrival, Sneh lived in the old zenana with Gulabo, whom she called her mother.

Sudha was not only beautiful and tall, with a slim figure, she was soft spoken and kind. She was also very liberal with her money. However, she refused to give her jewellery to Sumitra who wanted to keep it for her. The couple was happy and for some time Chaudhary Mohan Singh became a better man. Even his father lost his bad habits and curtailed entertaining the British. All this further lowered Sumitra's status.

Now my wife directed all her attention towards Sudha. The first step she took was to get more friendly and affectionate towards Chaudhary Mohan Singh. Though Sudha was carefree I was alarmed, and warned Sumitra to mend her ways. Then she called a new midwife from village Chattri and paid not only money but gave her clothes as well, in anticipation of the forthcoming pregnancy.

Sudha was very happy in the haveli but didn't like Sumitra

and Sneh interfering in her personal affairs. She often told Sumitra to find a good groom for Sneh. This made Sumitra angrier. When Sudha got pregnant, she went home to her parents for a few days. Chaudhary Devi Singh asked her to return and have the delivery in village Mauli. However she didn't, and there was some resentment in the family at Mauli.

A girl was born and she was named Rani. This infuriated Chaudhary Devi Singh, who was against having any female in the family, but Chaudhary Mohan Singh fell in love with the baby and she started growing up in the haveli. Chaudhary Devi Singh's illness, stroke and death gave Sumitra a chance to instigate Chaudhary Mohan Singh against the baby and Sumitra started taunting Sudha.

Rao Sahib heard the news and he took the baby to Rampur, where she was brought up by her grandparents. The presence of the baby at Rampur made Sudha go there frequently. This annoyed Chaudhary Mohan Singh and a minor rift developed between husband and wife.

In her absence, while under the influence of wine, he started entertaining Sneh and but for me it could have led to a disaster. I informed Sudha and she returned home. She was pregnant again and this time the dead female baby was buried in the labour room next to the barn by the midwife and Sumitra even before the mother could see her baby. Chaudhary Mohan Singh was told that the girl was born dead. This was enough for Sudha to lose her balance. Sumitra also started brainwashing the zamindar about an heir to the state.

I discovered that the girl was born alive and that Sumitra had told the master that too many girls in the haveli was not a good idea. He agreed and the girl was choked to death before the mother regained consciousness, and she was sedated to calm her. Soon Sudha started losing her balance. The news reached her father who came with a maid to look after her. Thus she came back to herself without the drugs.

This gave Sneh a chance to invade the zamindar's privacy and I laughed when Sumitra told the Chaudhary in my presence that Sneh was pregnant. This alerted Chaudhary Mohan Singh who was very scared of Dewan Sahib. He told Sumitra to send her to Kasganj and see that the baby was aborted. She was paid a handsome amount and both of them left the haveli. Sudha's third pregnancy brought happiness and this time her own maid looked after her. However just a few hours before the labour, the maid was drugged. The child was a male, but was declared a stillborn female, whereas Sneh's child was declared a male in Kasganj. When the maid came to her senses, she informed Rao Sahib because by now she was afraid for Sudha's life. Sumitra took the boy to Kasganj and only a placenta was buried in the labour room. There was sadness in the haveli but the news of a boy born to Sneh made Chaudhary Mohan Singh happy. He decided to accept the boy as his child and the heir of the state and asked Sumitra to bring Sneh back.

However, something went wrong with their plans because I picked up the drugged Sudha from the zenana and with the help of the maid took her to her room. The news of Sudha's sudden disappearance spread across the estate. The police came and after accepting a bribe declared the case of the missing zamindarin of Mauli closed.

With the help of the maid that night we took the unconscious Sudha out of the haveli to the temple complex and the maid looked after her there. Hanumanji's temple has an underground room and a passage made by Dhai Ma, which connected the room to Sudha's room. I learnt about this through Ramu who became a close friend of mine.

I knew my wife was so hungry for money and jewellery that she would visit the room at night, so I decided to take everything out before her arrival. I was successful, and all the jewellery, money, gold and silver were taken by us, leaving behind empty jewel boxes and velvet cases. Sumitra sedated Mohan Singh and entered the room with Sneh. Both looked for the jewellery but there was none. It was a successful day for me because I saw the disappointed faces of my wife and daughter. Rao Sahib arrived on the second day. Sudha was well but the entire village was surrounded by the police so we waited for things to calm down.

Within a month Sneh occupied the place of the second wife in the haveli. The son was declared as Sneh's and she and her mother started looting the money of the haveli. At this stage I told Chaudhary Mohan Singh to be careful or he would lose everything. The warning helped him, but both mother and daughter suspected me and the daughter was clever enough to try and poison her own father. You saved me but I become deaf and dumb and this satisfied them. I regained my power of hearing and speech within a fortnight, but decided to pretend to be deaf and dumb.

The son was only seven years old when Rani visited Mauli for the first time, but left on the same day because she preferred to stay with her grand parents and hated her father who caused the death of her mother. There was a saying in Mauli, 'The sinner progresses till God wishes and then gets his punishment.'

I found Chaudhary Mohan Singh keeping Sneh out of his room, but he was very fond of his son, Chaudhary Gujral Singh. At the age of six he sent him to Lucknow for studies and for years did not allow him to return home. During this time I took leave to meet Chhote Master at Lucknow. He was a real feudal, like an Englishmen – smart, and spoke English well. He told me that he met his sister and I told him what happened to his mother but not that she was alive.

Looking at Chaudhary Gujral Singh, I thought that now the haveli would be cleaned of the weeds growing inside. I discovered Gujral Singh's affair with Nirmala, Soni Devi of Rampur's sister-in-law. I wondered how the news didn't reach Mauli.

Chaudhary Gujral Singh told me that his father refused to attend the marriage because of ailing health and was scared of the interference of the two women of the haveli. I returned to Mauli and told Chaudhary Sahib everything. I saw his eyes shine and he blessed his son. His simple cough and cold became pneumonia and his condition started deteriorating.

One day at midnight he asked me to lock the door and increase the flame in the lantern. He dictated his will and I wrote. I was surprised that he had only one-third of the property he inherited from his father; the rest was taken by Sumitra.

As soon as I got the chance I told Chaudhary Gujral Singh how Sumitra, with the help of a lawyer and the young pandit who disappeared four days ago, put the thumb impression of the dead Chaudhary Sahib on the will. That will was read out. I told him that when I tried to talk to him, I was asked never to talk about the zamindarin. There were tears in his eyes when I told him that Sudha was alive when her father took her away, but beyond that I had no clue.

One morning Chaudhary Mohan Singh asked me to bring him tea. As I was about to go, Sumitra entered the room. I smelt a rat because it was the first time she had came to this section. I hid behind the curtain. What I saw almost made me kill this money-hungry woman but I waited. The man on the bed tried to get up but the woman pushed him back, and then asked him to sign a paper she held in her hand.

Suddenly I saw no movement and even the woman bent to check. She turned pale, then hurriedly put some ink on the right thumb and took its impression on the paper. She covered the man and put her hand under the pillow. When she failed to find what she was looking for, she locked the door.

She searched every nook and corner of the room but failed. This made me smile because the keys had already been given to Chaudhary Gujral Singh when I went to Lucknow to get his signature on the authentic will which was now with a lawyer in Lucknow. Failing to get what she wanted, she opened the door and left. I went to the bed and as I bent down, he opened his eyes and smiled, saying his behaviour was a drama. He took a promise from me that I would ensure his will would be executed.

As I brought in the tea for Chaudhary Sahib, Sumitra entered with a lawyer. She was shocked to see him sitting up and eating. The lawyer was embarrassed that he came without being asked, but said that he had come on Sumitra Devi's request. Chaudhary Sahib smiled, looked at Sumitra, told her to wait till he died, and quietly asked the lawyer to leave.

The rift between Sumitra, Sneh and Chaudhary Mohan Singh widened. Chaudhary Gujral Singh was asked to come from Lucknow and I was instructed to ensure that he was not poisoned. Chaudhary Mohan Singh had a sudden cardiac arrest which caused his death and that too on the day his son was due to arrive. Well that was the end of one generation and the beginning of another.

My role is to honour the will of the dead man; to weed the mother and daughter out of this haveli before leaving for Puri to be with my family again; and to beg pardon of my Lord Jaganathan. I remembered my father's words about the Bhagavad Gita. The three ways to develop God-consciousness are 'through karm yoga, jan janan yoga and bhakti yoga'. The best way as the Lord says is: 'Seek the path of devotion. Fix your mind on me, be devoted to me, worship me and make obeisance to me, thus linking yourself with me, you shall come to me.' This I promise I will do in the future and to live entirely depending on God.

***

'How is Chhote Sarkar?' asked the Vaid.

'He is busy meeting the locals. He and his sister, Rani, are together all the time. Though Sneh tried a motherly act, it didn't work. Both women keep a close watch on brother and sister and I on their food. Rani left yesterday after a talk with her brother. There must be something important because she was very upset when the police surrounded the temple complex. I don't blame her because her mother also disappeared like panditji,' Ram Dass said.

'Tea was served, after which Ram Dass took his leave and went towards the haveli. It was almost midnight and the streets were empty. I left and at the door of haveli before coming to you, I decided to meet Sudha. But my plan changed because I saw two figures coming from the rear suddenly hide behind the wall and then hurrying inside. I followed them but failed to enter. I was sure they were the mother and daughter so I changed my mind and decided to go to see Dhai Ma and Sudha. Somehow I had a feeling that they were alive and together. You know Ramia the soul does know and feel many things happening around,' Chaudhary Mohan Singh concluded.

The Eighth Day

'Ramia I am back after three days, visiting Kashi, Mathura and Haridwar. Let me tell you about my eighth day, which I spent at Kashi.'

***

Chaudhary Mohan Singh Learns about Kashi

I left at dawn, and though I am getting stronger every day, the distance was too much. I boarded a train at Faizabad. I was on the rooftop at first, but Ramia even that was crowded and no one appeared worried about the danger.

They were busy gossiping, sleeping and singing. There were no women or children. They were young and poor and had no ticket. I peeped into the VIP compartment. There was silence there, with everyone sleeping in comfort under fans. Each person had his own seat and there was no crowd. It was so clean and comfortable that I wanted to enjoy it, since it was my first train journey after several years. All the windows and doors were closed and there was not even a tiny outlet for me to enter, so I went to the over-crowded general compartment.

I took my seat in the corner away from the filthy, stinking toilet. The windows were wide open, yet the smell pervaded the entire compartment. Very few people were sleeping, they were so crowded together. Their eyes were closed but they were not sleeping. There was no place at all on any of the wooden seats, on the floor of the compartment and even in the corridor. Some wore only a dhoti, others were fully dressed and the women wore saris with their faces covered. Some were well dressed, but appeared resigned to the dusty place.

No one was fighting. By the time I entered they had probably organized themselves. I admire the way Indians make adjustment even in adverse circumstances. I wondered how they had arranged for over a hundred people, including sleepy children to fit into a space meant for thirty. These were the masses that have made and broken the National Governments of India since, 1947, while those in the VIP compartment occupy the seats of power. However those on an even higher level don't travel by trains these days, they fly.

I smiled at the thought of the common man – illiterate, living from hand to mouth, yet intelligent enough to make and break governments. Yes, we Indians are good in discussing politics, and criticising, but we don't fight for our rights.

The man next to me took a deep yawn and then started talking to someone sitting near him.

'Are you going to Kashi?'

'Yes,' the man replied. 'I am Mohan Srivastava.'

'And I am Srinivas.'

They shook hands like any gora sahib. I admired the British, though they have left, the English way of greeting is still used here. I am sure both men were pleased to prove that they were so modern and literate.

'Are you from Kashi?' asked Srinivas.

'Yes,' Srivastava replied, 'and we have lived there for many generations.'

'I am going there to place my father's ashes in the river Ganga, according to his last wishes.' Srinivas said.

'So you have never been to Kashi before?'

'Never.'

'Oh, you have missed visiting a most sacred place, which one must visit, more than once during his lifetime, and once more after death.'

'My father was a silk merchant and he was in and out of Kashi, but unfortunately I did not have the opportunity to go there.'

'Never mind,' Srivastava replied as though consoling him. 'Tell me about the city, the place where you were born and lived.'

This awakened the farmer next to me and he shook his wife awake to listen. Soon several heads turned to listen. On the floor or on the seat, the aim was to listen and enjoy rather than to sleep.

I remembered once Bhardwaj told me that if you ever travel and wish to enjoy it, do so by train because the people you meet and talk to, tell you about the real India. I waited. The man took a sip of water. Space was made for him to sit with both legs on the wooden seat and there was the silence of anticipation.

The man realized his importance so took his time in starting, while the others were waiting eagerly. It boosted his ego, and he wanted to enjoy this as long as possible, particularly as he was now sitting in greater comfort.

'Kasi or Kashi is also called Varanasi and Benaras. It is the oldest inhabited city in the world and has over 2,000 temples on the banks of the sacred river Ganga. The name Varanasi originates from two rivers – the Varuna and the Assi, which join the Ganga at the northern and southern borders of the city. However, it was earlier called Kashi or the city of light. The belief is that the first Jyotirlinga, the fiery pillar of light came up from the earth there and then flared into the sky.'

I looked at the farmer, who was so keen to listen, but he could not follow what was said about the light. He coughed and asked what the meaning of the light was. The man laughed and so did the others. He said simply that the light was due to the fire and smiled at his ignorance. His wife nudged him to keep his silence.

The man continued: 'That is the reason Varanasi or Kashi is called the city of light. The city is over 5,000 years old, because it is mentioned in the Mahabharata, the Ramayana and the Puranas as Siva's city. Those who die there are cremated at the burning ghats all along the river to attain moksha, meaning never to return to this earth.

'It is no wonder that saints like Sri Chaitanya Mahaprabhu, Lord Buddha, Sankaracharya and many others came to bathe at the Pancha-ganga (Pancgrada) Ghat. However during the early eleventh century several Muslim invaders looted this rich city.

'During the rule of the Mughals, Aurangzeb the last Emperor, destroyed most of the temples, which is why the existing temples in the city are not more than 300 years old. In the sixteenth century, in 1669 or 1670, the temples of Bindu Madhava, the Vishnu temple and Siva Visvanath were destroyed and mosques were built in their place.'

A man who was listening quietly, suddenly raised his head and commented, 'The Muslims, always try to harm our religion which is far more ancient, sound and well known.'

A man with a narrow face and well trimmed long beard, a Maulana, sat up and putting his feet down accidentally stamped the hand of a man sleeping on the floor. He said, 'You can't blame us Bhai Sahib. We are also Indians and have the right to pray in the land of our birth.'

This resulted in a sharp altercation between a man sitting next to me called Pandit Gauri Sharma and Maulana Shabhudin. The pandit's main objection was that Muslims say their prayers loudly when there is an arti in the temple of Kasi Vishwanath. The Maulana, who was initially in the mood to discuss this issue, suddenly stopped as he found himself alone. He probably thought that if he continued someone could beat him up or even throw him out of the compartment. So he decided to keep his silence and apologized to the man on the floor for accidentally stamping his hand in the heat of the religious discussion.

'Please continue,' a voice said from a distance.

'The river Ganga, which flows South-east towards Kashi reverses its course and flows north along the city. So you can imagine how auspicious this city is! There is a five-mile parikarma path which goes around the city.

'There are almost eighty-one bathing ghats and other holy kunds or sacred tanks. The most important cremation ghats are Mani Karnika, Dasaswamedha and Pancha-ganga. One must bathe at all three ghats to complete the Tri-tirtha Yatra. The others are Asi Sangam and Varana Sangam. If one bathes in all these places, he has performed what is called the Pancha-tirtha yatra. Those who go for the first time must bathe according to the ritual, which is first at Asi Ghat, Dasaswamedha Ghat, the ghat by the Adi Kesava temple near the Varana river, then Pancha-ganga and Mani Karnika.

'Following the baths at all these ghats, you must go to the temple of Kashi Visvanath Annapurna, and Sakshi Vinayaka (the witness canals). These days, devotees are lazy and visit all these places by boat. My advice to you is to do it on foot to get rid of this material body finally and end the cycle of repeated births and deaths; to seek moksha. You must also go to Adi Keshava Vishnu temple where the Ganga meets the Varana. This is where Tulsidas translated the Ramayana from Sanskrit to Hindi and a temple was built in his honour in the northern part of the town.'

The train stopped at a small station. A man entered with tea and the passengers each bought a cup of tea which was served with two biscuits. The tea was passed down from one end of the compartment to the other as though everyone there was one big family. Somebody mentioned that the station was Kashipur. This made me look around.

I remembered Dhai Ma was from here. I had an urge to leave the train and go to the zamindar's haveli.

'This place was very rich in silk production and the zamindar here was a very kind man,' the pandit said.

'There is no zamindari now,' someone remarked.

'I know but we all loved him.'

'What happened?' Mr. Srivastava asked.

'His only daughter Dhani Devi was married to a zamindar in a village called Mauli but she was tortured in her in-laws house. She left and went to Kashi.'

'What happened then?'

'I don't know. I left Kashipur years ago and am going to Kashi for the first time to live with my father who is now too old to look after the ashram.'

***

Chaudhary Mohan Singh Visits Kashipur

The train was about to start and an urge made me pass through the door, jump out and land on the platform.

The station was very small and there were just a few people who alighted from train. I looked around. A young man in his early teens was received by a middle-aged man. Though the boy was young he appeared dignified. I decided to approach them and what I saw almost took my breath away. The middle-aged man was a replica of myself. I went around him to confirm that it was not myself. Then I remembered that I was a dead man and laughed to myself.

There is a saying in the village that the presence of the soul of a blood relative creates an awareness and a sort of hollow feeling in his living relatives. I was surprised when this man in his expensive Western attire started turning from side to side.

The young boy asked, 'Father why are you so restless?'

So they are father and son I thought. I was still in a dilemma whether to go with them or carry on to Kashi when the voice of an old man made me turn. I was surprised to see the familiar face of Ramu, Dhai Ma's servant in the haveli, who also served me till Ram Dass took over.

I thanked the Lord and made up my mind to go with them. The old vintage car, a beautiful Red Ford, was waiting in front of the gate and the driver in his white cap and khaki clothes opened the door for father and son. Ramu, so old, yet healthy, after checking the three modern suitcases, took his seat next to the driver, while I sat in one corner.

The roads of Kashipur are bad and got worse as we drove through the interior of the town. It was 5 a.m., so there were not many people around, but those who saw the car stood on one side and paid their respects to the man. The small shops were closed; a man was arranging vegetables on a wooden platform; and of course there was a man selling newspapers.

On the outskirts of the town, the car took a turn down a wide road. Along the road were poplar trees interspersed with huge neem and pipal trees. It appeared to be a private road, and it was cemented. Throughout the journey, father and son kept their silence and so did Ramu.

Something must have happened as they were not in a happy mood. As we covered the miles and climbed the mound, we arrived at a palatial haveli, a combination of old and new wings. There were servants ready to receive them but the silence and sadness felt unbearable.

They alighted, climbed the stairs and reached the veranda. It was occupied by villagers. The man nodded to both sides, accepting their greetings with folded hands and then the huge door was opened. What I saw took my breath away. It was a big hall lit by a central chandelier. It had a red carpet on the floor and the two central stairways that led to a balcony on the upper floor. The walls were covered with family portraits in silver and gold frames.

The central part of the hall was occupied by a high platform where a body was placed on a white sheet, covered by a white shawl. The aroma of sweet incense filled the air and a pandit was reciting verses from the Bhagavad Gita in a melodious voice. There were a few women clad in white sitting on one side and an elderly gentleman near the body, close to the head.

Both father and son touched the feet of the dead person and then went to the head. They uncovered it and touched it. Both started crying and took their seats on either side of the older man. They sat quietly listening to the holy recitation. I went close and what I saw made me cry but there were no tears.

It was my mother, Dhai Ma, whom I had never loved till I discovered the true facts and that too after my death. She was old and grey and the face though fair had a blue tinge. The deep lines on her face showed the torture she had undergone, but there was also a glow of holiness. I stood looking at her and then looked around.

The portraits consisted of the zamindar and his family. One showed the girl in her mother's arms, another when she was four years old, holding her father's hand. Yet another was of her as a young girl in Jodhpur's sitting on a black stallion and there was one of her so beautiful and young in her wedding dress with my father, Chaudhary Devi Singh.

My father looked tall and handsome. It was no wonder that women fell for him. In a second I forgot everything looking at the handsome couple. I wondered what the fate of the haveli would have been if Dhai Ma had lived there instead of Sumitra. The last two portraits were of a young man in my grandfather's arms with Dhai Ma, and for a minute I thought it might be me, but I had never come here.

Then I remembered the birth of twins and in a flash realized that this was my brother; the brother who was secretly given to Dhai Ma's father. The zamindar of Kashipur lost his own son in an accident. The last picture was of a youth receiving a degree from the Principal of the school at Lucknow. So my twin brother was also educated at Lucknow and got a degree unlike me, who under Sumitra's influence, dropped out of school and lived as a zamindar with love for only women, wine and gambling. What a life!

As I continued to look around, I saw that the beautiful red and green brocaded furniture with cushions and several decorative pieces were pushed against the walls. It appeared that Dhai Ma's father was a rich zamindar and he lived like an Englishman. I climbed the stairs and reached the balcony that had a teak floor and led to a long, carpeted corridor with a suite on either side.

The woodwork, glass, carpets, fine lace and muslin curtains showed the wealth of the man and his grand style. The door to each room was partially open, according to the belief that the soul should be allowed to have a last look into the rooms of the house. One room belonged to my brother. It was very spacious; the floor was covered by a rich blue carpet, and there was a round double bed with a beautifully carved wooden bedpost. The bed was made and all the furniture was arranged on the side overlooking the green fields and distant hills.

Everything was expensive and the white crepe curtains were flying because of the open bay windows overlooking the balcony. There was a central portrait of Dhai Ma's father and a photograph lying on the side table of my twin brother, holding his black horse. He was in Jodhpurs, the typical dress we wore at Lucknow. On the other table was a photograph of him in his later years standing with Dhai Ma.

I was still busy looking at the room, when I heard footsteps and someone entering and closing doors. I peeped out and saw that someone was in the other bedroom. The door opened and Ramu came out holding a red sari and a jewel box. As he left, I entered the room. It was Dhai Ma's and everything she possessed since she was a child was persevered there. The bedroom was the same as the other one, except that the portrait on the wall was of Dhai Ma with Chaudhary Devi Singh after their wedding.

One side table had a photograph of father and son, me, and the other had one of mine with Sudha. I stared for a while and wondered at the love of a woman for her husband and her family. I was deeply engrossed when loud voices could be heard from downstairs. I went to the balcony and looked down. The body was now in the red sari and covered with a yellow silk sheet and flowers. They were lifting the platform on their shoulders while the young boy, now attired in dhoti and kurta, wearing a yellow turban was standing by the side. So this was Dhai Ma's grandson. I remembered my son Gujral Singh with a three-year old boy.

The memory made me proud, but I was scared of the two women in the haveli and the fate of my son in the near future. They chanted 'Ram-Ram' and the pandit holding a thali with flowers, incense and a diya in a silver container was followed by the people in the hall, while the twenty or so women stayed back. I followed the body down the mound to the bank of the river to an area marked 'Private Cremation Ground'.

The body was placed on a platform prepared with sandalwood. The pandit, reciting mantras, poured ghee on the body. The young boy lit the pyre. There was no crying now and everyone paid their last respects. I looked at the crowd and was surprised to see so many people. They started leaving as the fire reached its peak and the skull was pierced. I moved close to Ramu, who was crying.

Someone came to him and asked him when they were taking the ashes to Haridwar.

'Not Haridwar but Kashi, and I believe it would be at her father's samadhi, because that was what she wanted. So the zamindar is dead I thought. Then who was the old man? I understood, when Ramu told the man that Chaudhary Ram Singh has not left the haveli following his older brother's death last year.'

'Who is going?'

'Who but Chaudhary Dapinder Singh?'

'Why was the fire lit by her grandson when the son is alive?'

'It was her wish.'

Finally only Ramu, the son and grandson were left. For a long time they were quiet then the boy asked his father if his mother had the same rites performed here.

'No,' the father replied. She died in England soon after your birth, so I performed the rituals there, because it was not easy for me to bring the body here.'

'I am sorry Papa,' the boy said wiping his tears. The man consoled him by putting his arms around his shoulders. Silence prevailed and they waited till all was over. It was now dusk. Ramu collected the bones and ashes in a silver container and they left.

On the way back the man asked Ramu where Sudha was.

'She is in the ashram preparing for the ceremony to build the samadhi. Tell Dipu that she will be in Kashi because he wanted to meet her.'

The man nodded and they continued their walk to the house. So all was over and the Lord even showed me and made me participate in my mother's funeral.

I wanted to hear more about Sudha, but no one spoke till the ashes were placed in the centre of the hall in front of Dhai Ma's portrait. It was late, so everyone bathed and ate. The son and grandson then took their places on the floor on either side of the ashes.

When everyone went to sleep, I decided to explore the haveli. Next to the hall on the left was a big wooden door carved with silver and gold. I tried to remember where I had seen such handicraft before, but could not. The door was partly open. I entered and realized that it was the new zamindar's room.

It was double the size of the other two rooms. There was a big double bed in the centre and a sofaset was arranged along the side, half of which consisted of bay windows. The master must be very fond of white because except for the blue wall-to-wall carpet, the rich brocade bedcover, sofa covers, cushions and even the curtains were white. I looked around. The furnishing was a bare minimum.

There was a photograph of a family, and I was shocked to see Sudha holding a baby in her arms and my twin standing with Dhai Ma. It must have been taken several years ago because both the women looked younger. I wondered why Sudha was there and what her connection was here. In the centre there was a portrait of a very beautiful young woman, wearing heavy jewellery and smiling. But the portrait had a garland of silver and gold flowers. I guessed it would my twin brother, Dapinder Singh's wife. The bathroom was made of marble and every cupboard was closed.

I then decided to find out Sudha's secrets and her relationship with this man, the owner of the haveli, so smart and educated, yet so quiet and dignified, and with no vices. My brother, yet so different, owing to the circumstances in which we were brought up. A sudden jealousy blinded me, but then I came to my senses. I said to myself, 'I am a dead soul, so why should I bother?'

I went around the haveli on the outside. It had a swimming pool, tennis court, a barn for cattle and a stable for horses. I wondered at the richness of this state.

I left Kashipur with a sigh.

The Ninth Day

Chaudhary Mohan Singh Visits Kashi

I went to Kashi and wanted to take a dip before taking part in Dhai Ma's ashram rituals. All the ghats and temples are located in the old part of the city along the west bank of the Ganga.

As the man on the train had instructed, the first ghat I arrived at to perform the Pancha-tirtha, was Asi Ghat. It was dawn and there were very a few people at the ghat. I observed that the entire city was situated across the river on the west side. I heard a sadhu talking to a couple about the city and its origins. According to him seven ascetics built this city on an alluvial mound that had miraculously arisen from the river, which is why the city stretches only along one side of the river, while the other is a wasteland. To the south he pointed out a dense forest called the Forest of Bliss, with relics and sacred trees where sadhus and ascetics live with their disciples in seclusion after a dip, to pray and to attain moksha.

This city is as holy as Jerusalem in Israel, the birthplace of Christ. In short, it is a cosmogram, which is an intricate web of fifty-six pilgrim circuits. I believe the sadhu spoke the truth, because no sooner did I, a soul, touch the ghat, I felt as though I was reborn into a sacred cosmos. All my doubts, jealousies and bitterness vanished. The sadhu repeated the same rituals of bathing that the man in the train had described. So I decided to do the same. There was still time, so I started roaming and listening. The ghat called Mani Karnika Ghat was extremely overcrowded.

Usually a cremation ghat lies outside the city but this one was in the city. The river flowed by its side, but a man standing there told his wife that it owes its sanctity to a pool dug out by Lord Vishnu with his Chakra and filled with his sweat, where the Lord performed harsh austerities. When Lord Shiva and Parvati visited this place, Lord Shiva shook his head with pleasure and dropped one of his jewelled earrings, Mani Karnika in this pool, and that was how it was named Mani Karnika Kund. The saying is that it is so old that it was present when King Bhagiratha brought the Ganga to the city. There was a slab at the site, where cremations are performed for kings.

In front of the pool are the four steps of Vishnu. This kund is also called Chakra Push Kavini Kund or the Lotus Pond. In the olden days it was a lake. The kund is right next to the Mani Karnika Ghat and is surrounded by an iron railing.

A few yards away I saw the Tara Keshava temple. The deity is Lord Shiva who gives liberation. Relatives carrying the body of a dead person pass the temple in large numbers, and whisper a mantra in the ear of the dead person to ensure a good place in heaven. I saw almost half a dozen bodies being cremated while others waited patiently. No one was weeping because this was the only ghat where mourning for the dead was considered inauspicious. I noted how the dead person's eldest son's head was shaved and that he draped a white cloth around his body before lighting the pyre.

Following the cremation the relatives had dip in the river Ganga. The man on the train never mentioned the Mazdoor and Chandel Ghats, but these were some other cremation grounds. Chandal Ghat was named after the owner of the ghat, who was a Chandal, a caretaker by profession (the profession of cremating dead bodies). He was the one who gave Raja Harish Chandra the chandal's job and started living on his earning.

Though the ghat is now called Harish Chandra Ghat, the earning go to chandal, the first owner's descendents. One of the chandals told the mourners that these happenings occurred before Lord Ravana was born. Here the cremation ritual differed from the one at Mani Karnika Ghat in that they were accompanied by the beating of drums and dancing, but no weeping or mourning.

Ramia, I who used to be so obsessed about mourning for the dead lost my obsession. I liked the way they danced in time to the drums at every stage of the ritual. As chandal told the mourners, 'Why weep? Those who die return young, energetic and healthy. So we should celebrate their early, happy return to this earth.'

The majority at the ghat belonged to the rural and middle classes. They were religious and believed everything told to them. I wanted to tell them that I was a soul and would be here for thirteen days after cremation. So how can one be reborn so soon after death? What a myth!

I visited all the ghats – Asi Mani Karnika, Chandal, Panch-Ganga (the belief is that beneath this ghat the Ganga, Yamuna, Saraswati, Kirane and Dhutapuja rivers meet, and it is auspicious to bathe here during the night of the full moon of Kartika) and the Dasasvamedha. This is actually the main ghat for bathing and was overcrowded. The belief is that Lord Brahma performed a ten-horse sacrifice here for King Divodasa. So bathing here gives one the reward of performing the sacrifice of ten horses.

I also went to see the Sitala temple where humans undergo transmigration from death to life, and death again. All this satisfied me that I was not alone but I wondered, 'How many souls are watching their relatives at this very moment and why can't we see or feel each other?' This made me a staunch devotee of the Almighty, who keeps all the mysteries to himself and no one, even after death, knows about the others. The bells started tolling and I remembered the debate between the Maulana and the pandit regarding the temple and mosque. I remembered the famous temple of Kashi Vishwanath – The Lord of all.

From every ghat there was a lane leading to the city. The lanes were intricate and narrow and the houses on either side were small, there were cows and cow dung everywhere. I reached the temple of Kashi Vishwanath. It was now 5 a.m. and the temple complex was filling up with devotees. The entire complex was surrounded by a wall as though to separate it from the mosque next to it.

I entered through the small entrance bent my head to the feet of the most revered Jyotirlingam of the country. This was built by Rani Ahalya Holkar of Indore in 1776, dedicated to Lord Shiva, because the old temple was destroyed by Aurangzeb in 1669. It is called the Golden Temple because Maharaja Ranjit Singh had gold plated the roof of the altar. The lingam is also placed on a golden altar. A 10,000-year-old temple of Lord Shiva is also seen here, and on the left is the statue of Lord Vishnu. I saw a small black stone lingam set on an altar of solid silver. Like all temples, the air was filled with the thick aroma of incense and devotion, and the tolling of bells. People were standing around another shrine which was protected by a grill – on a cloth-covered pedestal was a deity with a large silver mask and a splendid Rajput moustache, draped in dozens of marigold garlands. The area around his feet was sparkling with thousands of clay lamps.

The devotees were calling out: 'Shani Maharaj ki Jai'. Shani Maharaj or the planet Saturn troubles people unless they placate him. They accepted the water of the Jnanvapi Kund or the well of wisdom from the panditji. The belief is that the well was dug by Lord Shiva, to cool Vishwanath's lingam. The water was clear jnana (water), which leads to liberation after death. The well was also covered by bars. One bucket is taken out daily to distribute amongst the devotees before they enter the temple to clean their eyes before looking at the lingam.

There were sounds of Allah next door and I felt sad for those who cursed the Muslims. But why should they create conflicts by praying aloud while the prayers were said at the temple. It was past 7 a.m. I wanted to see Dhai Ma's Ashram and be there before the arrival of her ashes. But how? I did not know the whereabouts of the site.

As I was wondering what to do, I saw a blind beggar sitting outside the temple gate. I went to him and whispered, 'Where is Dhai Ma's Ashram?'

The man answered, 'Go to the left and then left again and you will reach a dead end where you will find the ashram. It is waiting today for Dhai Ma's ashes. It is a sad day for me. She was a great woman.'

The child sitting next to him said, 'Baba why are you talking to yourself?'

'I am not.'

'Oh Baba!'

'I am not senile, someone asked me a question.'

'All right. Take this prashad I got for you from the temple.'

'Thank you,' he said and started eating.

I felt sad and wanted to give them something but I had nothing with me. During my entire life, Ramia, I never took any interest in the local people of my village. How they lived in adverse conditions when there were droughts and floods, whether they had even one meal a day. I never bothered about their naked children and half-naked women in torn saris in summer and winter, because I only wanted money. However what is the use of repenting now when I am a soul, helplessly waiting for the thirteenth day to leave this earth. And where will I go? I don't know Ramia. I don't even know my fate, but I am not scared to face it.

I followed the blind beggar's instructions and reached the ashram. It was on a mound, a white building which was once the exclusive bungalow of Kashipur's zamindars. It had the best of furnishings and comforts, and with beautiful lawns, flowers and fruit trees. It overlooked the flowing river below with its wondrous ghats and the marshlands across the river.

A man in a uniform was sitting outside the gate, looking at the main road. I knew he was waiting for the family to arrive at 11 a.m. for the samadhi ceremony to be held at the site overlooking the Mani Karnik Ghat, according to Dhai Ma's last wishes. These were her words to Ramu because her son, my twin brother was not there when she took her last breath.

I entered the gate, walked straight to the house, climbed the stairs and finding the main door open, I entered and mingled with several other people, who were going in and out of the house, busy with the arrangements for the burial ceremony of Dhai Ma'a remains. The hall, unlike the Kashipur haveli was small, but the staircases on both sides were as majestic as they were in the haveli, ending in a balcony overlooking the hall.

There at the top I caught a glimpse of a woman in a white silk sari, whom I thought could be Sudha. However she turned and left the balcony. I sat in one corner because now the hall was full of Ma's devotees, sitting on the carpeted floor facing a huge statue of Dhai Ma. The white marble statue resembled her living figure exactly. I marvelled at the artist's talents. The panditji entered and he started singing devotional songs, but the figure in the white sari didn't join the crowd.

After a while, Ramu entered the hall and went up. This was followed by the sound of vehicles outside. The doors were opened wide and the servants started rushing around. It was the new zamindar, my twin, holding the silver container. He was in white kurta-pyjama and shawl and his head was covered with a cap. The young boy entered wearing similar clothes and they walked up to the central place where the former placed the container.

I saw a figure in white coming down, her face was covered

by her sari. She went up to the container, bent down, touched it and took her seat next to the young boy. I was sure it was Sudha. The young boy gave her a ring. She looked at the older man, who turned and nodded, and she put the diamond ring on her right ring finger. I just couldn't understand this gesture and was more confused about Sudha's relationship with this family.

I looked at the woman who was once mine and whom I had treated so badly. All the years of torture hardly seemed to affect her. She was now more elegant and smart, with a peculiar glow on her face. I realized how strongly I was under the influence of the two women – one a nautch girl and the other a eunuch!

It was a short ceremony and then everyone stood up. The young boy held the container and the older man and Sudha like a couple on either side of him put their left hands on it. The panditji covered the container with a marigold garland and started reciting mantras.

The boy led the procession to the site where a deep hole was dug under the well-built white canopy of the shrine covered on top but open on all sides facing the flowing sacred river Ganga. Here the urn was buried with religious rituals and covered by the three with dust. They were joined by Ramu who was especially asked to do so by the master.

Ramia, I realized that my mother received from her other son, my twin brother, what I failed to give. Even though I was sad, as a soul I was now satisfied to see that everything was done correctly. The people were served food and the poor were given clothes and money before the family of three left the ashram leaving the rest to Ramu. I stayed back, because I was keen to learn more about these two women – Dhai Ma and Sudha. Somehow I was convinced that Sudha had become a part of this family long ago.

Ramu guided the workers on building the stairs and covering the shrine on three sides with glass and the side looking down to the river left open with a wide bay window.

At dusk he returned with a few women and men holding a silver thali with flowers, incense, a sacred diya and some fruits. He offered these at the small marble slate over the buried urn and the prayer started, lasting for almost an hour. I looked down and saw the busy ghats of Kashi. I wondered why Dhai Ma didn't want to be cremated there to attain moksha. Then I heard a woman asking Ramu whether the new zamindar would marry Sudha to fulfil Dhai Ma's ambition. Ramu nodded yes.

He sat next to her on the stairs and then said, 'I was close to her when she entered the haveli, but she kept her silence. Together we built this ashram and then Sudha arrived. Dhai Ma listened to everyone but never uttered a word.'

'You're right she was a very private and determined woman. That is how, even after her death she brought Sudha close to the family and she will now be the new zamindarin of the haveli. He remained unmarried for ten years after Kunti's death but now there will be some happiness for him and the boy. The boy loves Sudha so much. He was brought up by her after they returned from England. I am sure she will be very happy and she deserves it.'

'Let us eat and then, Roma Devi, I shall tell you all about Dhai Ma after she left her in-laws house.'

***

Ramu Talks about Dhai Ma after Her Departure from Mauli

Dhai Ma left Mauli at night because she feared Sumitra, who had already hired three men to kill her. Sumitra was determined that her niece, Sneh, should marry Chaudhary Mohan Singh and that she should kill Dhai Ma and steal her jewellery, money, silver and gold.

When we arrived at Kashipur her parents welcomed her but when they discovered that she had left Mauli permanently, her mother couldn't bear the thought of the effect this would have on Dhai Ma's son – one of the twins adopted by the her parents. He was due home from Lucknow for his wedding, which was arranged with the Raja of Kashi's elder daughter, Princess Kunti. The princess was an educated and religious woman. She was also good looking and had a melodious voice. The young couple were to be married in a hurry because the boy was soon to go abroad for a three-year law degree. This upset Dhai Ma, who thought that as the only daughter of her parents, they would take care of her.

That night she expressed her resentment and told me she was glad she did not have to depend on her parents during the years of torture she spent at Mauli. She asked me to accompany her that very night, and we left the haveli for Kashi. But she did not go to her bungalow; she went to the ashram near the Forest of Bliss, which was mainly meant for widowed or deserted women.

She shaved her head and wore a saffron sari to live in disguise. The ashram gave her a two-room hut where we lived. I started serving her, and she served the other women living there. Periodically, she brought the ashram to the attention of the country, because of the handicrafts she introduced, her welfare work and the old people's home she set up. Before the head of the ashram, Swami Ravi Nand died, he appointed Dhai Ma as the next head. I went occasionally to Mauli, where Ram Dass was the zamindar's personal attendant.

Dhai Ma found out about her son's wedding and mother's death from the occasional letters written by her father, and from newspapers. Her father asked her to return, but she never replied. Then she discovered that her father had died and left his entire property to his only daughter, Dhani Devi, and after that to his grandson. The news didn't deter her from her mission.

Then came the bad news that Kunti had died in London and left a newborn baby. Her father told his grandson

Dhai Ma's secret and asked him to look for her. Thus when he died, Dhai Ma's son placed a notice in the newspapers requesting his mother to return to look after the family. I showed this to Dhai Ma who was now suffering from ill health. She didn't reply. I had maintained my connections with Ram Dass and he informed me he had rescued Sudha and handed her to her family at Rampur.

After the death of Dewan Sahib's wife, he remarried and the stepmother insisted on Sudha returning to Mauli even though her father protested. I told Dhai Ma and this news made her active. She sent me to Rampur and one night I brought Sudha, who was too sick to walk, to Kashi. Here the women of the ashram looked after her and she regained her health.

When Sudha recovered fully, Dhai Ma revealed her entire story to her and insisted she work as a governess to her grandson at Kashipur. When I took Sudha to the haveli, Karan Chand, the old servant recognized me. Sudha was taken to Mauli in disguise occasionally, to see her children. She wrote to Dhai Ma that she wished to leave, but Dhai Ma did not allow it and so Sudha stayed on. After some time, she began to forget her past, and concentrated on looking after the baby, Dipu.

Sudha was in her late twenties, but looked younger. Even though no one dared to look down on her, Dhai Ma was worried, more so when Dipu was five and was sent to Lucknow. Sudha asked Dhai Ma if she could leave, since the master was posted to the High Commission in London.

Karan Chand discovered Dhai Ma's address through Sudha's letters and informed his master. One night when Dhai Ma was fighting for breath due to acute asthma, I was about to go out to get a doctor, I opened the door to assess the cold and found a man standing there. He didn't give me a chance and pushed himself into the room.

The meeting between mother and son was heart-rending and she suddenly collapsed. Thus she was taken to hospital and from there to her house in Kashi. The son nursed his mother day and night and slowly she recovered. The resentments of the past were forgotten. I went to Kashipur and brought Sudha to the house and she started caring for her. Dhai Ma regained her health and then opened the house for the women of the ashram, so that they could live in better hygienic conditions. She gave the old ashram next to the river to a mazdoor to create a cremation ground for the poor.

Prem Kumar, a mazdoor came to Kashi many years ago to cremate his wife. He was refused because he didn't have the money to pay for it. He set the body aside and begged for three days to get enough money to cremate his wife. This made him determined to create a new cremation ground next to Mani Karnika Ghat for poor people like himself. He became a beggar once again and requested Dhai Ma to keep his money safely, till it was enough to fulfil his mission. Dhai Ma encouraged him and with this money and Dhai Ma's help he was able to fulfil it.

The ghat was inaugurated by Dhai Ma and named the Mazdoor Cremation Grounds. Here any poor person even with only a rupee can have a cremation performed. Sudha took over the housekeeping at Kashipur.

The master of Kashipur was posted outside India and Dipu spent most of his holidays with his father. However his love for Sudha, whom he called aunty, was intense and this gave Dhai Ma some hope, as she wanted her son to return to the haveli and settle down with Sudha.

Then one day she had an acute asthma attack and her son and grandson came down from Kashipur with Sudha. I noticed the way Dipu hugged his aunty and the way the master observed them. The master gave up his job and settled down with his mother at Kashipur. What happened between mother and son I don't know, but I noticed that she no longer wore her diamond ring. She knew that she wouldn't live long and was prepared to return to Kashipur.

Here after so many years she went to her room.

I saw a sudden change in her health but she told me she would not live long. She called Dipu and told him her last wishes in Sudha and my presence. She asked Sudha to go to Kashi to make the arrangements for the last rites and asked me to get all the rituals organized according to her wishes. She told me how much she loved her parents and never wanted to marry and then she choked.

Looking at me she smiled, blessed me and said, 'I gave my ring to my son and told him through Dipu to get Sudha's nod to marry her. Ramu he confessed his love for Sudha to me but was too scared to ask her. I told Sudha to fulfil my wish whenever someone gave her my ring. She is a funny girl; she cried and nodded yes.'

***

It was now dark, yet the ever-awake ghats, busy with transmigrating souls, were alight. Ramu got up and said, 'Be ready for the new zamindarin because I saw the ring on her left ring finger.'

He smiled and taking slow steps entered the ashram with the woman who could not walk fast because of her arthritis.

I touched my mother's shrine and left. However the woman who was just behind asked if the wedding would be performed soon.

'No.'

'Why?' She asked.

Ramu replied, 'I am going to Mauli tomorrow to get the old zamindar, Chaudhary Devi Singh's skull. It was stolen by a ghori from the cremation grounds. A young pandit, Gauri Sharma, who was taking tantric lessons from an old ghori, helped to steal the skull, that too before it was pierced. The chhote zamindar did not even bother about it when Ram Dass informed him.'

'That means Dhai Ma's husband is piccassa (an evil soul who has no liberation)!' exclaimed Roma Devi.

'Yes. That is why I am going there in disguise and Ram Dass will help me get the skull. We will take it to the Ganga where the grandson will join me for the pind dan and the soul will leave this world as pitre.'

'How long ago did Dhai Ma know of this?' She asked.

'It was only after Chaudhary Mohan Singh's death, when the ghori tried to steal his skull, which was saved by Ram Dass. He was sure the reason the ghori tried to steal his skull was because Sumitra wanted to make Chaudhary Mohan Singh her slave.'

'When are you going?'

'I must reach there by tomorrow, before the will is read, because I believe in the strength of the ghori's mantra recitation on the skull of Chaudhary Sahib. This will lead to the end of the young zamindar. I fear for his life.'

They entered the ashram and I decided to go with Ramu.

An old man wearing trousers, a half-sleeve shirt, jacket and hat came out after an hour. He was holding an expensive bag and looked like a retired government officer. He boarded the first class reserved compartment of the train and I sat next to him. It was cool inside and the seats were cushioned. A man even came and spread clean, washed sheets and soft pillows for everyone. Ramu ordered tea and went to sleep.

Most of the passengers had seats for themselves. Some were served food on trays and others ordered cold drinks. They did not talk to each other and within an hour the lights were dimmed and everyone was asleep. I reflected on the different levels of people in this country. There are the downtrodden; the educated, poor and struggling; and then the higher classes. Looking at Ramu, I smiled and admired his devotion to the family. Such people are rare and deserve a good life. I was happy that Dhai Ma looked after him well.

I recalled the diamond ring worn by Sudha. I had no regrets. She had character and during her youth she either fought or cried, while I closed my eyes to those two women's nasty tricks. I remembered Ramu saying that a tantric can close the mouths of mighty kings, so Chaudhary Mohan Singh was nothing for him.

Now I realized how I would get confused when Sumitra was there. Even when I heard about the will I wanted to fight, but accepted it when she touched me and in a soft voice asked me to accept it.

I remembered how I saw my daughter being suffocated but couldn't utter a word. Sudha's patience gave way and she said she had not fainted, but lay quietly because she feared she would be killed. I remembered my relationship with Sneh. At first I doubted if she was normal, but later, it appeared as though I was under the effect of some drug. Ram Dass warned me but I couldn't make up my mind.

As I looked back I thought that she was manlier, unlike Sudha. It was too late now to repent, so I waited to reach Mauli with Ramu or Babu Ramu! The journey was dull compared to the one in the crowded compartment. So I left the cool compartment and entered the over-crowded general one, just in time to help a man who was in deep sleep by preventing a young boy opening his small box. I nudged the man. He got up and caught the boy. Poor fellow he was almost thrown out on the platform half-dead when the train stopped.

A man in a long saffron robe with long black hair and beard was reciting mantras. However, I suspected him because periodically he would push a bag under the seat. I went down close to the bag and what I saw alarmed me. There was a small human inside the bag struggling for breath. I was helpless but I nudged a woman sitting next to the sadhu. I continued till she looked down to see who was pushing her and then she shouted.

A young man looked down and brought out the jute bag. When he opened it, we saw a four-year-old, semi-conscious boy. The sadhu tried to rise but the crowd overpowered him and revived the boy. The boy said that the sadhu gave him a biscuit and then he was not aware of his surroundings till he was revived by the other passengers.

The sadhu was handed over to the police with the boy at the next station. When the train started there was a discussion on sadhus. A man called Narinder Deva said that one should never talk against holy men as one never knew where one would see the Lord. Suddenly he had an ardent audience. He started talking about life after death. Some rishi munis, after severe penance got salvation and freedom from the cycle of life, death and rebirth. He extolled his audience to do good deeds to receive the rewards of good karma, but janam was a must.

They say after death, the soul goes to pitra loka. Here it awaits judgement and is then reborn in some form. This could be for several hours or several years. Here in this world one is close to one's relatives and at times the attachment is so intense that they are reborn in the same family. However, those who live here must know that the right rituals can liberate the soul as pitra and not pittar, which you can become after an unnatural death or when rituals are not carried out.

The train slowed down and everyone got ready to leave. I decided to get back to Ramu, while thinking that my father was pittar and wondering how to release his soul.

The Tenth Day

It was past 4.30 p.m. when we reached Rampur. Ramu hired a rickshaw and gave the man directions. I sat next to him and the man started peddling. On the way the man told Ramu that the Dewan Sahib's second wife was very ill and there was a rumour in the town that she was dying.

'How is the old man?' Ramu asked.

'He is healthy but it is sad that he lost both his daughters because of this second wife who was so cruel to them. She wanted to keep everything for her son from her first marriage but there was a train accident two years ago and the son died. This made Sheila Devi a better human being, but by that time she had not only lost her husband's love but her two stepdaughters who never returned.'

The rickshaw stopped in front of a palatial mansion by the side of the main road. It was a small town, and everyone knew about everyone else's private lives. It was the same in Mauli.

There were no lights on in the mansion and everything was quiet. Ramu got down and rang the bell at the gate. The gatekeeper came out from a small hut and asked his identity. Ramu asked for the Dewan Sahib after disclosing his identity.

The gatekeeper left him and went inside. A light came on in the veranda and the old man returned. The gate was opened and Ramu followed the man up the stairs to the covered veranda to enter a well-furnished sitting room where the old Dewan Sahib was waiting for him. Ramu touched his feet and was about to sit on the floor when the old man asked him to sit by him. The Dewan Sahib sat silently, with tears falling down his cheeks. Ramu consoled him.

'Dewan Sahib I heard your wife is very sick.' He nodded. 'I have come to tell you that both your daughters are well and Soni Devi's grandson is with Mauli's Chhote Sahib.'

The depression lifted. The old man smiled and almost touched Ramu's feet for bringing such good news. He rang the bell and after asking for refreshments, started talking to Ramu.

***

Shri Narayan Singh, the Dewan Sahib of Rampur Tells his Story

I was born in Haldwani where my father was a cook in the family of Lala Gopal Chand, a shopkeeper. I was the only son born after several years of marriage, so my father wanted to give me a good education. Thus he moved to Rampur.

The Nawab of Rampur was very fond of kababs and this was well known in the state. My father opened a small dhaba. He started selling kababs and was soon renowned in the city for his tasty kababs. As a small child I helped him and soon our lives changed. I was put into school and being good in studies throughout passed high school with flying colours. Ill fate suddenly took my father's life. He died of a heart attack and I had to leave school to look after the dhabha.

Here I met Bano, a maid in Nawab Asif Shah's zenana. She introduced my kababs to the palace. I was called by the Nawab Sahib and asked to take on the job of the head cook of the palace. Those were the days when nobody dared oppose the ruler's orders. So I had to close my dhabha and take the job. I came to the attention of the ruler and from cook I was asked to become an accounts officer and then made the Dewan of Rampur. My mother wanted me to marry her distant relative, Sheila, but I refused, being ambitious and under the influence of young Bano Bi.

However, to please my mother and to avoid the controversies involved with a Hindu-Muslim relationship, I married Sheila. She was the best wife anyone could ever have, but for five years there was no issue, so I adopted a two-year-old daughter of my colleague, and named her Soni Devi. Then within a year my own daughter Sudha was born, while Sheila died during childbirth. I raised my two daughters with the help of my mother and then came the shock.

One night Soni Devi disappeared. On asking my mother I was silenced, but I continued the search. Since my mother was not keeping good heath, Sudha was married in a hurry to Chaudhary Mohan Singh. Poor Sudha had a tough time. My mother died and then I was foolish enough to bring Bano Bi disguised as Ram Dulari as my second wife. To tell you the truth I will take this folly with me to my pyre. When I heard about Sudha's miserable state in Mauli, I wanted to bring her here for proper treatment.

Soni Devi's husband, a young teacher with whom she had eloped, was also poor. I decided to help her, but Bano Bi threatened to expose me if I ever helped or brought my daughters home. Soni Devi's husband died. I sent money but it was returned, because she had left with her one-year-old son, Dinesh Singh. Then Sudha came to our house but my wife almost threw her out during my absence.

Today my wife is dying, and her son, for whom she discarded my daughters without my knowledge, is no more. Ramu, I am happy that she is leaving this house because for ten years this woman sucked my blood like a leech and I was quiet only to maintain my reputation.

***

Ramu said, 'I am going to Mauli and on my return I shall be back with Dinesh.'

That was when I realized that Dinesh was not my grandson. I wondered what the reason could be to lie? However, it didn't hurt me.

'He is three years old,' Ramu continued, 'and Soni Devi is in Dhai Ma's Ashram at Kashi, coming out of her depression. Sudha is to wed Chaudhary Mohan Singh's twin brother. You know Chhote Sahib will turn out to be the best of the zamindars of Mauli and I am going there to help get rid of those two women occupying the haveli.'

Ramu ate some food and then left Dewan Sahib. He was happy to give Sudha's father news about her, and see the father look optimistic that all would be well in the future. He reached the gate when the gatekeeper told him that a car was ready to take him to Mauli. It was an old car and the driver was a young Sikh boy. Ramu took his seat at the back and I sat next to him.

The car sped along till we reached the main road, which was supposed to be a highway, but was in bad shape. 'We have our own government, but there is still no sign of progress anywhere.' Ramu went to sleep.

I reflected on my life. I came, stayed like a dumb man in the hands of two women and then died, again with the help of my so-called grandmother, Sumitra. I remembered how she entered my room.

I was gasping for breath and asked Ram Dass to bring water. She sat next to me and asked for the keys. When I couldn't reply she covered my mouth with both hands. I recalled how I tried to fight for my breath and she asked again and I nodded. However Ram Dass entered but by that time I had no idea of what happened, because I was fighting for breath.

What a life! I wished as a soul that the Almighty would let me return to the same haveli so that I could repent the sinful past forced on me by those two women.

There was a sudden jolt. Ramu opened his eyes and asked the young boy how far it was to Mauli. 'Not very far now but why are you going there? Mauli is a part of my past too. I was born and bred in the quarry across the river. Dewan Sahib saved some of us but my parents are still there working day and night for one meal a day, living like animals and being beaten.'

'Who is the cruel person who does this?'

'The zamindarin Sumitra Devi and you can witness it yourself.'

No one spoke further till we reached the outskirts of the village. There the boy stopped the car, got down, spat on the ground and told Ramu to get out of the car because he refused to go near the haveli; his blood boiled whenever he heard Sumitra Devi's name. Ramu got out but not before a man clad in a white sheet came out from behind a tree and stood near Ramu. It was Ram Dass, who was waiting for him.

There was no one in the temple complex. We walked around the clump of trees famous for the nag devta's presence, till we reached the pipal tree. Here Ram Dass turned left and moved a big stone lying near the roots of the tree. He tapped it, and to my surprise a small door just large enough for a man to crawl into opened. Ram Dass entered, followed by Ramu.

Stairs just narrow enough for one person to climb, led to a room lit with gas lanterns. They climbed carefully down to the room. A man was lying next to a young boy, and he rose as we entered. Both men touched his feet and sat on the ground. Gujral Singh asked, 'How is my mother?'

'She is well Sir, and sends her blessings to you,' Ramu replied.

The words made his eyes misty but he controlled himself. 'All is well,' both men spoke together.

'I hope so! To tell you the truth, I am too sick even to look at these two women here.'

'You must wait a few days longer,' said Ram Dass. We must plan for the child to leave and Dewan Sahib is anxious to have him. He told me his story and it was sad that a man had to fight a woman who was a Muslim maid. She blackmailed him, which is why he kept quiet.'

The news of his step-grandmother, a Muslim, alarmed the young master and he told Ramu that Dinesh would not go there. However hearing that she was on her deathbed, he agreed to leave Dinesh with Dewan Sahib till he was ready for school. Then Ram Dass suddenly started and looking around, recited a mantra.

I knew he felt my presence, so Ramia I left the room through a small hole near the wall and waited outside the haveli. I saw Gujral Singh enter the haveli. I followed him. He barely reached the room, occupied by his father earlier, when there was the sound of footsteps. The door opened and Sumitra with a maid holding a tray entered. She asked the maid put the tray down and leave and sat on the bed.

'I was waiting for you. You must not miss your meal,' Sumitra said and gave him a glass of milk, but the young man politely refused. She then told him about the arrangements she had made for the pind dan ceremony on the thirteenth day.

'I could not find the keys to the safe. I wonder whether they are with Ram Dass because he was there when my son died,' she concluded.

'The keys are not with me,' the man said.

'I am now satisfied that they are in safe hands as his will is with me,' she said, watching the young man's face. Noticing no change in expression gave a sigh of relief. She knew now that she could get anything written on the blank paper with the thumb impression of the dead man.

'Your father loved Sneh very much and I am sure, like my husband, all will be well for her. I pity the young boy Dinesh spending so much time with adults. He should be taken care of in the zenana. I am sure Sneh will come out of her depression in his company.' The young master didn't reply and yawned; a sign for the woman to leave. As she got up, I decided to go with her.

***

Chaudhary Mohan Singh Reports on Sumitra Devi and the Ghori

Sumitra entered the zenana and went straight to her daughter's room. Sneh was eating and talking to the maids. Sumitra was shocked because she knew these women would gossip about the widow eating fried food even before the thirteenth day ceremony was performed. She asked the maids to leave and whispered her anger to Sneh who ignored her and kept eating. This angered the old woman and she lost her temper but before she could say anything, the younger woman left her food and glared to her mother – a warning to stop nagging. This had an effect on Sumitra and she stopped talking. Sneh finished her meal and sat next to her mother.

'Did you get the keys?' Sneh asked.

'No. He said that he came after his father's death so did not have a chance to take the keys.'

'Who can have those keys? There is one possibility: father.'

Sumitra paled and recalled how he favoured the young master. She wondered how she could get the keys from him. She was in deep thought when Sneh said, 'You didn't help Guru Maharaj to get the Chaudhary's unpierced skull, otherwise his soul would have been our slave and told us all the secrets.'

'I couldn't because your father was guarding the pyre and he showed his loyalty to the young master by making a noise when the pandit and the ghori went there.'

'Then don't worry and let us meet Guruji today. He will solve our problem.'

The sudden expression of relief on the old woman's face made Sneh happy and she got up but then stopped and asked her mother about the boy. 'I asked him, but he didn't come out of his daze.'

'Mother, you know Guruji will not be very happy.'

'I know but I was helpless and also scared. Over a period

of three months, six children have disappeared from the village and the quarry owned by our zamindari. If anyone suspects us we will be in trouble.'

'Yes, but all is well so far. I wanted to go there but was scared of my husband who had no clue about the quarry, the forced labour of the landless and the lucrative amounts given to the manager Prem Nath. Let us first take over the estate and then we will manage the rest. Our first aim is to get rid of my so-called son and then tame my father, so that we become the rulers – the two the rich women of Mauli.'

There was no point in staying on, so I left and went to the mardana. Ram Dass told the young master that once they get Chaudhary Devi Singh's skull, they would take it to Gaya where his son, my twin brother, would perform the pind dan after which the soul would be pitra and leave for pitra loka.

'Ram Dass you felt the presence of a soul in the room but did not say anything further. Why?'

'I felt the presence but could not decide whether it was Chaudhary Devi Singh or Chaudhary Mohan Singh.'

'Can you call a soul?'

'Yes!'

'Then why don't you call my father's soul?' The young master asked.

'I can but I won't as I promised my father when he gave me the mantra. He told me never to call a soul before it reaches pitra loka. So I am sorry I will not call the soul.'

The young master decided not to press him any further and silence prevailed. I decided to leave because I was scared of Ram Dass's tantric powers.

Sumitra Devi left her daughter's room and entered hers. I followed and was surprised when she locked the door. She opened the safe hidden behind the curtains. She took out the jewel box and to my utter surprise it was the one that belonged to Dhai Ma.

She took out each piece of jewellery and placed it on the

bed. I saw Sudha's heavy diamond and ruby necklace. Sudha once told me that Sumitra had borrowed it, but never returned it. I recalled how I scolded her for telling a lie and accusing an elderly woman. She returned all the items to the box except the necklace and two bundles of notes, which she put into a paper bag. Then she left the safe open and placed the box in the cupboard. I was still watching her when there was a knock at the door. She replied that she was tired and sleepy. She then placed the two blank sheets of paper with my thumb impression inside the safe. She pulled out some clothes from the cupboard threw them around and went to bed.

I left and sat on the arch of the haveli gate. Somehow I was feeling restless. There was a change in me and I had gained strength. A pandit arrived for the routine recitation of the Bhagavad Gita, but I was in no mood to listen. To tell you the truth Ramia, I was sad to leave this earth.

At midnight I saw two fully covered figures leaving the haveli. I knew they were none other than the mother and daughter. I followed them. Taking quick steps they entered the forest and walked quietly till they reached the middle, when one of them brought out a torch. They walked as though they knew this part of the land well and I could see no fear. Then I saw a cluster of trees and as they crossed it, the scene changed. Next to the bank of the river there was an open space and a fire was burning in the centre, in front of which sat a man in a long black robe wearing many beaded necklaces, his head covered with black cloth.

He looked up and his eyes were red and angry. He was the ghori. Sumitra had told me about the power of these sadhus who live and meditate in cremation grounds. They capture the souls of the dead with mantras by obtaining their skulls before they are pierced by the Brahmin, while the pyre is burning. Through this soul, which remains pittar they get their work done and keep it forever as their slave. My blood boiled as I remembered the sins this man had performed with my father's soul.

Both women threw off their white sheets and sat across the fire after touching his feet. Sumitra called him Guruji. She placed a small bundle wrapped in a paper bag in front of the man who took out the heavy necklace and money. He was pleased.

Then in a husky voice he asked. 'Where is the boy?'

'I couldn't get him,' Sumitra replied.

'That is not good but never mind, on the thirteenth day, the last ceremony will be over and the will read out.' 'Where is the will?' the ghori inquired.

'As far as I know there is none and as you advised, I suffocated him and got his thumb impression on the blank paper,' Sumitra said.

'Go to the lawyer Hari Mohan, who is my disciple, and ask him to do what is necessary.'

Sumitra rose and touched her Guruji's feet. He gave her a drink in a bowl. She drank and sat down again. When Sneh did the same, he held her and asked Sumitra when she would fulfil her promise. Sneh struggled but he forced her to drink the same potion.

As the women prepared to leave, he whispered into Sumitra's ears. She nodded and touched his feet again. They left the forest and I followed.

Along the way Sneh said in a husky voice, 'Look Mother, I won't come here alone. I don't like him.'

'You liked Chaudhary Mohan Singh?'

'No. I hated that drunken zamindar but he could never molest me because I drugged him with wine and he didn't know I was a eunuch.'

'A eunuch who bore him a son,' Sumitra said, and they had a good laugh.

They reached the haveli and entered through the back door. The younger woman went to her room and I followed Sumitra. She opened the door, lit the gas lantern and then saw the clothes scattered all over the room including some expensive pieces of jewellery. I looked at the bed. It belonged to my mother but everything was taken over by this woman. She increased the gas and under the flame she saw that everything was set.

She started screaming and lay down near the open door. Sneh came running. She had not changed as yet. She sat next to her mother, looked around and called the maids and with their help put her mother on the bed. Sneh surveyed the scene and told the maids to see if they could catch the culprit. She revived Sumitra, but looking at the empty safe, Sumitra fainted again and asked Sneh to rush to Guruji. Sneh left her mother to a trustworthy maid and ran out of the haveli. I followed her.

Ramia, this was the first time I saw her manly power. She ran swiftly to the place they had earlier met the Guruji. To her surprise he was not here. She shouted. A stark naked man came out of the river. He dried himself, and wrapping a sheet, around himself stood in front of her. He put his left hand over her mouth, picked her up and took her behind the bushes to a thatched roof hut.

He threw her on the bed and as he was about to close the door, I entered. I admired the ghori's lifestyle. It was a comfortable bed but the rest of the room was empty. He tied Sneh's mouth with a black scarf and carried her struggling down the steps to a well-lit spacious room. There was a beautiful comfortable bed in the room which was covered with carpets and cushions on the floor. There were bottles of wine in one corner with silver glasses and plates besides expensive pieces in the form of silver and gold ware, and locked cupboards and boxes in another corner.

He threatened to kill her if she made a noise. This worked. He filled a glass with a red drink, unmasked her mouth and forced the liquid down her. He also started drinking. The drink soon sedated her. He took off her clothes and then his own and what he saw made him laugh.

'So you are in a true sense a eunuch!' he said and roughly took her in his arms and started kissing her.

I turned my face away because I couldn't watch the unnatural sex act, as by now Sneh complied with whatever he wanted. Her rear passage was bleeding when he finally stopped and ordered her to leave.

Her naked body was covered with just a sheet as she ran and the man laughed without shame. It was dark but nearly dawn. She entered the haveli and went to her room, closing the door violently.

***

Ramia, I left the haveli and came to see you. But I must leave at dawn. Ramia did you know that she was a eunuch? I saw her naked for the first time having unnatural sex with the ghori. The only thing I wanted to confirm was Sumitra's part in the drama. She was lying comfortably on her bed drinking milk while a maid was pressing her legs. I was too stupid, even when Sudha remarked on Sneh's unusual voice, way of walking and gestures. She told me her doubts but I was under the effect of Sumitra and the ghori's mantra.

Today, as I talk I wonder at my stupidity. But all is lost now and I am a dead man. However, if she suffocated me to death, then please tell Ram Dass to have my pind dan done at Gaya, along with my father's.

I must go now, but we will meet tomorrow.

The Eleventh Day

'Ramia get up. Listen to the news I bring. This will kill the two women and at last my son will be the sole owner of the zamindari of Mauli.'

Ramia opened his mouth to tell him about the dead pandit, but then decided to keep quiet and listen to the soul.

'I left you at dawn and went to the forest. There I saw two men sitting under the shisham tree. I had a laugh seeing Ramu dressed in Western clothes and Ram Dass as his servant. I sat on one of the branches but kept away from Ram Dass. Ramu told Ram Dass that soon after a female figure left the ghori's hut, he arrived there.

***

Ramu Meets the Ghori

I rang the bell. There was no reply so I rang again. Then I saw a black man on the left. He was almost six feet tall and wore a long black robe. His head was uncovered, showing his long hair which was tied back at the nape of his neck with a black thread. He was somewhat unstable, but sat drinking a cup of nectar, the so-called holy water.

I told him I came from Kashi after hearing about him, a renowned Guru. I said that my second wife, a nautch girl, was unfaithful to me but I loved her. So I came here to get a potion from him which could make her my slave. At this, the man laughed and told me it was not free. I said I was a rich man and could give thousands for my Ram Pyari.

'How much?' he asked. I replied that I would fulfil his demand. He gave me a figure of ten thousand rupees. He would perform the ritual in front of me and send me home with the potion, after which his captured slave would help me. I showed my surprise at the mention of a captured slave.

'Who is your captured slave?' I asked. He didn't reply, but gave a sneering laugh and told me to come at 10 p.m. with the money. I nodded and I am waiting here till then.

***

Ram Dass told him to wait till he returned with food. He showed him a hiding place behind the bushes very close to the flowing river. There was silence after Ram Dass left. I woke up when the man returned holding a basket.

Ram Dass awakened Ramu, who had fallen asleep and they ate without speaking. There was still an hour to go, so Ram Dass left and Ramu went to sleep again.

I heard a soft whistle and became alert. Beyond the clusters of the tall trees someone came out. It was the young pandit. He looked around then went to the river threw water over himself, though he was still clothed, and chanting mantras walked towards the village. I followed him.

He went inside the temple complex, unlocked his room and locked it from the inside. There was a knock and as he opened the cupboard, I saw a sliding wall and then, what I saw surprised me. It was Sneh, looking very pale. She narrated the happenings of the previous night. The pandit listened carefully and then told her to wait till she became the zamindarin of Mauli. They ate some food and she gave him the blank papers and told him to get lawyer to do the work according to Guruji's instructions.

The man nodded and then started making love to her but there was a knock on the door, so Sneh left and the cupboard was closed. Ram Dass was standing at the door when it was opened. He asked the pandit to give him the papers so that he could deliver them to the lawyer as suggested by Sumitra Devi. It was decided that both of them would go together when it was dark. I was really angry with Ram Dass, convinced that he was with his family. However I didn't know how to inform Ramu and Gujral Singh, my son.

***

Ramu Steals the Skull from the Ghori

I left the temple complex and went to Ramu. The fire was burning and I saw a skull lying on the hot ashes. The skull was plastered with saffron and tied with a red thread. It was intact, there was no hole and I knew it belonged to my father. The ghori, now attired in a fresh black robe, head covered with a black scarf started reciting and occasionally making Ramu, in his Western attire, touch the skull. This went on for some time and then the ghori gave some ash and the thread to Ramu and told him to put them under his wife's pillow.

The ghori offered him wine, which Ramu refused. He handed over the money and rose to leave. However, the ghori told him to wait till he brought the potion from inside. He left the place with the money.

Ramu quickly picked up the hot skull, put it in the bag and ran fast. On the way he met Ram Dass and I knew this was a well planned mission. He would have failed if Ram Dass was playing a double game.

As they came out of the forest I saw the same car with the driver waiting. Ramu held Ram Dass's hands, bid him good-bye and asked the driver to drive fast.

Ramia, I was elated at the thought of seeing the ghori's reaction. So I returned to his hut. He was restless, searching the hot ashes looking for the skull. He looked helpless. Then he closed his eyes and recited mantras but no one came with any news.

***

The Quarry

Across the river I heard someone crying. Ramia, across the river beyond the cremation grounds, next to the ghori's hut I saw what I never ever expected to see in Mauli. It was a quarry. There were about ten children aged five to seven or more, but so malnourished, almost naked with matted hair and dirty bodies busy working in the mud while seven women and about ten men in the same state were making bricks.

You'll be surprised to know that your older son, his wife and two children were also there. I realized that they were all Dalits and as I went close I recognized them. They were Kulu, Hildu, Omu and Dilu of our village, though I was told they had left the village and gone to Mumbai. They were working like machines. What I saw further took my breath away.

A child of three months suddenly cried and when the mother left her work to give him milk, I heard a shout and you'll be surprised to know who it was. It was the young pandit Gopal now wearing Western clothes and holding a whip. He whispered something to the woman and when she told him the baby was theirs, he laughed and picked up the baby to throw it to the ground. This alarmed the woman and she fell to the ground but that did not bother him and he threw the baby on the bricks. The baby fell listless while the mother fainted. None of the other workers even glanced at them.

He called out to Kalu, a tall, ferocious, naked man, who came out from one of the huts. He had a blunt knife in his hand and it looked as though it had been used many times to kill. He went close to the baby and told the pandit that he was dead. The man laughed and told him to bury the child. He picked up the body as though carrying a rabbit in front of all those living corpses and crossing the river arrived at the cremation grounds.

He dug a grave, cut off the head with its hair and buried the rest of the body. There was a sound of footsteps and guess who arrived? The ghori. He picked up the head, laughed and patted the man for his work.

'That man took the old man's skull, but this skull will also work,' the ghori said.

'How many skulls do you require?' the man called Kalu asked. 'The graves of all these children and those of the Muslims are headless because of you. I wonder how they help in your tantric work.'

The ghori was silent for a while, then he shouted at Kalu and I saw the heavy, well-built man falling at the ghori's feet begging for pardon. He made him get up, then asked if there were any new additions.

'No,' Kalu answered.

'Why?'

'There are now seven missing children and even though you ate their flesh, the bones in the river are human bones and if anyone were to investigate this we will be in trouble,' Kalu replied.

'You're a coward,' the ghori said holding the skull and asked Kalu who was next!

'Guruji, Bilu's girl is only four years old, she is the only one left but if you have sex with her, she may die.'

'Don't worry. Bring her to the hut at midnight.'

Ramia if I was human I would have killed him but being a soul I kept my silence. I felt even Kalu was working under stress. I followed him back to the quarry. A bell rang and the children and adults went to the river to clean their hands and drink water. Each of them was given two dry chapattis with one onion and a paste of red chillies. They ate and after hardly an hour, were asked to get back to work.

In the hut I saw the pandit and Kalu drinking, and two young boys, almost naked, standing. They were your grandchildren Ramia. Both were crying but quietly and I saw the signs of whip marks on their bodies. I went to the other two huts where all these people were lying on the bare ground. I heard your son whispering to his wife but she closed his mouth while sobbing. Ramia I won't be here but it is your duty to get not only your son but all the others out of this dreadful place.

I heard someone crying. It was none other than the mother of the young baby. I went to her. Ramia I couldn't comfort her so just whispered in her ears to tell me the truth and I would help. She looked around and then started speaking in whispers. However the cry of two boys beyond made her hide her face in her lap for a while and I saw her trembling from head to toe. She then controlled herself and started talking.

***

Beena's Story

My name is Beena, the youngest daughter of Kirpal Lal Gupta, a bania from village Kaurali next to Mauli. I was studying in high school when I met this so-called young pandit Gopal in the temple complex. He was very charming and I fell for him. He promised to marry me but then one day he called me at night for prayers to Hanumanji that he conducted every Saturday night. He also asked me to bring money and jewellery. I stole some, reached the temple complex and hid myself. When everyone left, he took me behind Hanumanji's statue. He pressed something and the statue moved to one side. Lifting a stone he told me to follow him. I saw a staircase in the dim light. He closed the entrance and guided me down to a room.

I come from an average family background, and this room was well furnished with bed, cushions, carpets and everything was made of gold and silver. There was a wine cabinet with silver glasses and a small kitchen where some food was ready. We ate and as I decided to go home he insisted on my staying. I refused but then he insisted on my having a soft drink with him. I agreed and after that I was not aware of what happened.

When I opened my eyes I was on the bed stark naked and next to me was Guruji, the ghori. I looked at myself and knew that all I had was no more. I was now a woman with no respect so I decided to leave the room and inform the police.

However, the man got up, caught me near the stairs and gave me a beating. For three days I was virtually kept prisoner. For three days the ghori assaulted me and I didn't see Gopal, the pandit. I was so weak when Gopal came that he started making me drunk. I was pregnant and was kept a prisoner until I delivered a child.

At this stage I was taken out and placed as a worker in the quarry. I worked and bore all the humiliation for this child but now I am going to end my life.

***

Ramia, I tried to console her and she asked me who I was.

'Never mind, I am hiding behind the wall so tell me,' I replied.

'Every woman, man and child is a victim of these three men. The boss is Guruji and even though Sumitra Devi owns the quarry, almost every penny goes to Guruji,' she continued.

'Do they pay the workers?'

She gave a hollow laugh. 'Yes, one sari a year, a meal of two chapattis with red chilli paste and river water to drink; water from the river that contains human bones.'

'Do they eat human flesh?'

'Yes,' she said, 'and they drink water in human skulls.'

There was a sound of steps and someone said that a woman was talking.

'It must be Beena in her madness,' and the laugh was cruel and sarcastic.

'Tell me one thing,' I said. 'Gopal came to Mauli only after Rattan's death. How did he team up with Sumitra and the ghori?'

'After he escaped from Kaurali jail he changed his name, grew his hair and became a priest of the Hanumanji temple in Kaurali. That was when I met him.'

I promised to help and she looked around and asked, 'How?'

I told her to wait and see. I left her weeping for her son and entered the hut where amongst others, your son, his wife and their two sons were sleeping. They looked like the sleeping bones of a human skeleton. The hut was bare except for one earthenware container with water and a small mug alongside. I hurried to tell you to save your son and grandchildren.

'Ramia don't cry.'

'And all the while I accused my selfish son of enjoying life in Mumbai. Will the police help?' Ramia asked.

'Wait for a day and then go to the young zamindar, Gujral Singh. Tell him what I told you and ask for his help. Ramia I must go but do as I say. Let the new zamindar get his rights after my departure on the thirteenth day.'

'All right Sire. Beena's father is dead but her mother is alive and so is her brother. It is said that they also called the ghori Guruji and when her bhabhi couldn't have a child the ghori treated her and she had a son. However, now I know whose son that young boy is!' Ramia laughed.

'Do you know this pandit?'

'Yes. He is from a butcher family and came to Mauli as a disciple of the ghori. He then entered the haveli and under Sumitra's patronage became the chief pandit of the temple complex,' Ramia replied.

'How do you know him?'

Ramia laughed. 'I used to visit his father's shop for my dog and knew young Gopal or Gopi as he was called earlier. His father admired him because he excelled in cutting meat. Young Gopi was money-minded and in order to get his father's shop he killed his brother, but got caught. He escaped from jail and later became the ghori's follower. After Rattan's death he was made the temple pandit.'

Ramia continued, 'I was shocked to see him at the temple and that he was so close to the haveli. Even your puja is being done by him, a butcher.' Ramia spat on the ground.

'I tried my best to keep away from this man. When you told me that Rattan was dead I thought that he would survive. He is also a cat with nine lives. Even his body has not been found and I am sure he must be hiding and will be appear at the appropriate time. That is what I wish to tell you,' Ramia continued, bitterly.

'Your bitterness moves me but I am helpless. I have two days left, and wish to tell you everything I see and hear. But you are feeling sleepy and there is an hour left for dawn. I couldn't control myself and shouted. The strength, the change in me and the strong voice make me wonder. To tell you the truth Ramia, I feel a day here is equal to a year of growth of the human within me.'

***

Ramia, Oh Ramia! Wake up. I may be seeing you for the last time. However, I am happy that my son will be the next heir to the Mauli estate. I regret doubting Ram Dass' integrity when I saw him sharing food with Sumitra and Sneh. I saw him giving Sumitra the keys of the safe and sharing his secrets about how he wanted to make his family the heir of this estate. They were all laughing while eating.

Then he told Sumitra how he and Gopal would go to the lawyer's house to get the will made officially and declared on the thirteenth day after the ceremony.

Ram Dass said, 'I lost the best opportunity when the zamindar asked for tea and I left. When I returned I found him dead and you and Sneh were crying while the maids were looking on. I had blank papers but it was almost impossible to get his thumb impression.'

There was a silence, then Sumitra rose and brought two sheets of papers from the cupboard.

'When did you get this impression?' Ram Dass asked.

'When you left and he was calling you. I tried hard to get his signature or thumb impression but he refused so I suffocated him in anger. He died,' Sumitra replied.

She didn't see her husband's face, which wore a peculiar expression, and continued that he must get everything done legally. Ram Dass nodded and after drinking his tea rose. He asked for some money. Sumitra gave him a bundle of notes and hugged him. I was sure that he was one of them, so felt sad, but didn't know how to tell my son. Then I remembered that the man helped Ramu steal my father's skull and leave the village. This thought gave me some consolation and I decided to follow him.

He left the haveli and sitting in my car, asked the driver to take him to Kaurali. He knew the driver Kushwant Gupta was Sumitra Devi's close associate. Everyone in the haveli is under her grip because of her ruthless cruelty and money. Just near the temple complex the car stopped and Gopal joined him. No one spoke till they reached Kaurali.

Gopal then gave directions to the lawyer's house. He told Ram Dass that Sumitra Devi wanted Sohan Lal, her lawyer, to get the will legally accepted and then he asked for the money. Ram Dass gave him the bundle but it was lighter than the one Sumitra had given him. 'I think the money may be inadequate for this job,' Gopal said.

'You're right, but she said the rest would be given once the work is complete. She also wished to have one copy today. She is very clever and wise,' Ram Dass said smiling at Gopal.

'Yes, but I don't trust her. Such women don't even spare their own blood relations,' Gopal mumbled.

'You shouldn't talk like that about her,' Ram Dass said convincing the driver of his loyalty to the lady of the haveli.

'I agree,' Gopal said, changing his tune.

They arrived at a narrow street where the car couldn't enter. They walked to the lawyer's house to meet the man who changed Chaudhary Devi Singh's will, so that his son then owned only one-third of the original property. It was sad but then the woman had guts and was cunning and bold enough to do anything to get the remaining land. A deep sigh alarmed the pandit, who asked Ram Dass what the problem was.

'Nothing,' he replied, 'just a thought.'

The rise and fall of the zamindars of Mauli was in the hands of two women and Gopal laughed, 'You're right and to tell you the truth, I am tired of performing wrong deeds. After I killed my brother, I wanted to become a pandit to pursue good karma for the future.'

'You should be grateful to Guruji and Sumitra Devi.'

Gopal nodded.

'Where is Rattan?' Ram Dass inquired.

'He lives with Guruji but he has lost his voice and is an invalid.'

The lawyer's house was small but well built and looked in good shape. As soon as they reached the gate, a short, fat man came out as though he was waiting for them. He took them inside to a room which seemed to be his office. It was dingy and had a minimum of furniture. He asked them to sit, while he opened a cupboard and brought out a file. He picked up two papers with official markings. Then he looked at Ram Dass and said, 'You have come from the haveli?'

'Yes.'

'Where is the money?'

Ram Dass took the bundle from Gopal and placed it on the table. The man counted the notes and said that there were three notes less. Ram Dass put his hand inside the bag, found the three notes and gave it to him. The man smiled. He put one paper in the file and started reading the other:

'I Chaudhary Mohan Singh, in the presence of my grandmother and wife make this will and the lawyer Kirpa Gupta must write as I dictate. It is my wish that the entire estate including the haveli will belong to my wife, Sneh, but the overall administration will be under Sumitra Devi's control as long as she is alive. Sneh cannot sell anything or do anything against the wishes of my grandmother Sumitra Devi. To our son, mine and Sneh's I give rupees twenty thousand because I spent thousands on his education in Lucknow. The money will be given by Sumitra Devi only after he signs that nothing in Mauli belongs to him.'

The lawyer stopped and then showed that the will was signed and dated a month prior to the death. He gave the paper to Ram Dass and told him to give it to Sumitra Devi, adding that he would be present at the thirteenth-day ceremony.

Ram Dass saw that Chaudhary Mohan Singh's signature was perfectly copied. He looked at the lawyer and asked, 'When did you get his signature?'

'I didn't. A man named Kalu, the manager of the quarry copied it, in the same way as he copied Chaudhary Devi Singh's signature.'

'Which quarry?'

'Don't you know?'

'No,' Ram Dass was perplexed. Then Gopal told him to keep quiet till everything was finalized, after which he would take him to the quarry.

The lawyer was suddenly alarmed when Ram Dass said, 'I have a paper with his thumb impression, which would be more fool proof.'

'No, this is better, because Chaudhary Mohan Singh was an educated man and the thumb impression could cause more doubt,' the lawyer said and Ram Dass nodded in agreement.

Putting the envelope in an inner pocket, Ram Dass with Gopal left the house. On the way, Gopal told Ram Dass that he wondered how Sneh, a eunuch, could produce a child.

'How do you know she is a eunuch?'

'I shall tell you the truth. I started an affair with her for her money but am required to continue even after I found out that she was a eunuch,' Gopal said and laughed.

Ram Dass didn't reply but he was hurt that his own child

was going around with a man like Gopal just to enjoy life. He felt helpless. They reached the city, ate some food and drove back to the village. He gave Sumitra the will and told her to destroy the paper with Chaudhary Mohan Singh's thumb impression because the lawyer didn't approve of it.

She took the will, her face glowing with happiness and in that state of mind, she gave Ram Dass another thick bundle of notes.

It was dark when I followed Ram Dass again. This time he walked to the outskirts of the village and hired a rickshaw. He arrived at the house of Bishambar Dass Gupta, another lawyer of Kaurali. He knocked and entered the house. The lawyer was sleeping, but awakened and took him to his office. Ram Dass narrated the happenings of the day and asked Guptaji to be at the ceremony with the genuine will and the keys the late zamindar gave him. The man nodded and told him not to worry because this time everything was done well in time and legally. Just then a maid entered and told them that a woman from Mauli wished to see him. Guptaji was surprised and told Ram Dass to go to the other room. Ram Dass left, but kept the door ajar to hear the conversation.

The woman and a tall dark man entered the room and closed the door with a bang. She asked her companion to lock it. Bishambar Gupta, a respected lawyer of the local court, sat at his desk. The woman removed her burqa and it was none other than Sumitra Devi. She sat down and asked the man across the table.

'Do you have any letter from my late grandson?'

'No.'

'Look, you step outside and my guard will take you to an unknown place where you will not even get water,' Sumitra Devi said in a threatening tone.

'I have not got any letter,' the lawyer said now feeling rather shaky.

'Kalu, go through his papers,' and then turning back to the man said, 'Just be ready for the consequences if I find anything against me.'

Kalu started searching through the files and papers in the cupboard. The woman sat waiting like a statue. The man finally turned and told her there was nothing in the room.

'I know you came a month before my grandson's death. What did he talk to you about?' she asked in an authoritative tone.

'He told me he wanted to write a will and would call me again. But the call never came.'

This satisfied Sumitra Devi. She got up and before leaving warned the man not to come to the thirteenth-day ceremony, as he had done on the previous occasion. 'Remember what a beating you got from my men the last time. One lawyer is enough for the family.'

The man didn't reply and the woman, satisfied with herself, left the room quickly.

A car could be heard driving off and then there was silence. Ram Dass came out of the room. 'Where were you?'

'Behind the curtains and this is the file and keys.'

'I am glad you took the file otherwise I would have been in trouble. She is a ruthless woman and can do anything for money.'

'I think you should keep the keys and file because a lawyer is coming from Lucknow and I shall stay away but you must come as witness.'

'I must have protection if I am to attend the meeting after the ceremony,' the lawyer said.

'You will. I will be there and she is scared of me,' Ram Dass said. 'I shall straighten her out physically in the morning before the ceremony, and all will be well.'

The man nodded and Ram Dass touched his shoulder to reassure him.

***

Back at the haveli, Sumitra asked Kalu whether he saw any files belonging to the zamindars of Mauli. Kalu said that he had not.

'Do you mean there wasn't even a file cover there? That means the lawyer has hidden the file in some other place.'

'I don't think so,' Kalu replied. 'The lawyer is too timid. He knows he will die if he interferes in your affairs and he is scared of you.'

'Gujral Singh must die. Suffocate him like his father and grandfather tonight,' she said and took a deep sigh. 'I am sure this lawyer was hiding something from me. So the only heir must leave this world.'

I was alarmed and went to my son's room. He was not there. I looked around. The safe was locked. I waited, but when the door opened, Sumitra entered. She looked at the unslept bed. She locked the door and opened the safe. To her horror it was empty. Her face paled, she locked the safe again, left the room and went to Ram Dass' room. Her husband was not there either, and she was still thinking when Ram Dass entered.

He was surprised to see her in his room after so many years, so he hid. Sumitra was turning the room upside down but couldn't find anything. She left and entered the zenana. Sneh was waiting for her even though Kalu had told her everything.

'Did you get anything from the safe?' she asked.

'It is empty. I carried out Guruji's magic over the last one year and I saw that it was not working on him. The late zamindar was getting more interested in his son in Lucknow. I am sure he sent everything to him there.'

'Do you mean money and jewellery?'

'That is not my main worry. My worry is that he may have made another will. Even though he had only one-third of the property, if the will favours the young man, he will live here.'

The door opened and Ram Dass entered. Sumitra showed him the keys and told him that the safe was empty. Here the man acted superbly and showed his innocence and ignorance. Ramia I really felt good about such a man, who has such integrity and self respect. 'How did you get to the safe?'

'Earlier we had decided to suffocate the young man, but then I gave it a serious thought and decided that he can be killed by other means after the ceremony. However, he was not there so I opened the safe, but it was empty.'

'It could not be the son, so who could it be?' asked Ram Dass.

Sumitra said, 'I don't know, but I got these keys from the dead man's cupboard soon after his death.'

'When the young man occupied the room, he didn't ask me anything about his father's death, papers or keys,' Ram Dass said.

Just then Gopal entered saying, 'Guruji has lost the skull. A rich businessman came for basikaran (to make a person a slave with the help of tantra) and when Guruji went inside the hut to get the potion he vanished with the skull. Even Beena has disappeared and can't be found.'

Ram Dass, acting perplexed asked Sumitra who Beena was. She told Gopal to leave, sat down on the bed with a deep sigh and started crying. Ram Dass knew her act and in the past it worked, but he was no longer the same man. He too decided to put on an act and started consoling her, assuring her that he would be there for the family. This satisfied her and she relaxed.

Ram Dass acted well and gently stroking her hair asked, 'Whose skull was he talking about?'

'They think it was the skull of Chaudhary Devi Singh but even Guruji is wrong.'

'Why?'

'Chaudhary Devi Singh is alive and counting his days in the dungeon meant for smugglers below the haveli.'

'I can't believe that!'

'You can see it for yourself,' she said.

This news shocked Ram Dass but he waited. He decided

to be silent and not ask about Beena, because he had rescued her at my son's request after you spoke to him, Ramia.

'Leela, a maid in the zenana is the illegitimate child of Chaudhary Devi Singh and Kanta, the daughter of Chaudhary Vikram Singh of Shampur, a small village in the Terai near Nainital.' Sumitra started.

'They had an affair when he visited Nainital. She was beautiful and very timid but she loved Chaudhary Devi Singh dearly. They got married in a temple at Nainital when the young zamindar was only nineteen. He promised to marry her officially in Mauli, but later decided to obey his parents to get more money from Kashipur and married Dhani Devi.

'When his young wife almost discarded him because of his love for wine and women, Chaudhary Devi Singh came to Gulabo's kotha. I met Kanta when he was courting me. This new woman brought money and jewellery to convince him through me to marry her because she was pregnant. I agreed but I had my own plans. She gave birth to a girl and a boy whom she named Leela and Kalu. She died within a month of the delivery.'

Ram Dass admired her for being so smart, telling these lies to her own husband. But he listened with patience.

'I left them with Gulabo Devi when I shifted to the haveli. At the age of twelve I brought them to the haveli because Gulabo was too old to look after them and Sneh. Guruji became my close friend and mentor and together we explored each and every part of the haveli to smuggle hashish and find a place for unwanted bodies till they could be disposed of.

'One day, young Kalu, who hated his father and blamed him for his mother's death, and Gopal came to my rescue. He picked up the drugged, sleeping zamindar took him to a room and kept him prisoner. Kalu arranged to feed him and occasionally even tortured him,' she concluded.

'Is he really alive?' Ram Dass asked.

'Yes. Come, I shall show you Chaudhary Devi Singh whom

I visited to make him sign a will. However the old man is tough, which is why the will had to be forged,' Sumitra explained.

'Who was the man who died as the zamindar?'

'One of the bonded labourers from the quarry.'

There was a silence and in her excitement, she told her husband that the grandfather and grandson would be in the dungeon together, while the rest of them would enjoy the booty of the rich land and haveli.

'Smuggling hashish also brings money.' She laughed like a child and hugged Ram Dass who responded by pretending to be keen for more love from her and the money which belonged to the young zamindar.

I left and went to the dungeon. I knew about it, but was convinced by Sumitra that it was closed after the death of Chaudhary Devi Singh. I was also convinced that all wicked dealings during my father's life, like female infanticide, rape, smuggling of hashish and so on was stopped by Sumitra Devi.

Three months before my unnatural death I asked Ram Dass about the police inquiry regarding hashish in Mauli and he came out with the facts. Earlier I was convinced of the love given to me by the two women. Ramu warned me and Ram Dass came to my rescue. So Ramia, how can I leave this mess even as a soul, knowing about the quarry?

There was a silence; then Ramia said, 'You must discover the facts. I am sure as a soul you can help by warning Ram Dass about the facts you will come across'.

'It is dawn so I must leave. We will meet tomorrow.' Ramia nodded.

The Twelfth Day

RAMIA WAKE UP and listen, I am so excited. I saw my father Chaudhary Devi Singh and now I am sad to leave this world but I have to go. Even though it was early dawn when I left you, it was dark because of the clouds, and the streets were empty. I entered the haveli but the door to the dungeon was locked. Then I remembered a tunnel opening into the river bed. Once, as a child, I entered it with my friend Kishore.

It was dark and the river was full of water, but we walked through the tunnel and arrived at a hall filled with men powdering some dried leaves. No sooner did Munshi Pratap Gupta, whom I called Gupta Uncle, see me he turned pale and within seconds we were taken out via the staircase up to the haveli. He left us in the small attic leading to the men's section.

The next morning my father was told, and he gave me a stern warning not to ever go to the riverbed and within a short time I was sent to Lucknow to the prestigious Talukdar school. Life was good, full of the comforts of living in British style, but I was not interested in studies. My interests were riding, swimming and eating good food. There I heard that after my mother left, Sumitra Devi took over the Haveli.

However, I was so busy enjoying life that I did not bother about Mauli, till high school and then I got bored of studies, left school and came home. Here life was full of entertainment, wine, gambling and freedom to do anything, as I was the only son of the zamindar, and Sumitra helped me at every step to get me into a worse state every day. Savitri Devi had no say. Sumitra was my real grandmother.

After my marriage to Sudha I sobered down, but Sumitra's influence remained, and wine, women and gambling became my way of life. Following my father's death, whom I never blamed for putting Sumitra in charge of the zamindari, I was the head in name only. The people of Mauli did not accept this and they advised me, but I refused to listen.

So, yesterday, Ramia, I entered the hall through the riverbed once again. It was dark but the tunnel was lit with gas lanterns. This surprised me because not only was it lit, it was also clean. The entire hall was occupied by cardboard boxes. Then I heard the sound of sobs. I listened and found that the sounds came from the central room.

The wooden door was locked. The sobs stopped and someone started coughing. The cough became persistent and it sounded as though someone was gasping for breath. The door next to the room opened and a man came out. He unlocked the door and as he entered, I went inside. There was the most unbearable smell of filth. He lit the gas burner and under the light I saw a haggard old man reduced to skin and bones with a long white beard and equally long hair, uncombed and matted. He was in a dhoti and was sitting on a bed of hay and in the corner there was an earthen pot with a filthy mug.

The young man was none other than Kalu and he was angry. He pulled the man by his hair, forced some water in the mug down his throat, kicked him with his left foot and told him to lie down and not make a noise. The old man did nothing, but the huge red eyes that looked at the young man showed his hatred and I knew that he was my father.

The man left, leaving the door open and called out to someone to clean it. I waited and then there was a knock. The old man made space in his hay bed where he was sitting. What I saw surprised me. The stone in the floor slid back and I saw a hole large enough for a man to crawl out of. The face of a woman peeped out. She gave him a bag and said, 'All is well, she has no fever but she is worried about you. You must eat the food, throw the bundle into the hole and then go to sleep.

He nodded and I saw a smile between the long beard and bushy moustache. He opened the bundle. The dried bread and cold vegetables made him feel hungry. He ate and drank the water and then hearing footsteps, threw the bag into the hole and covered it with hay. He was so quick that I knew my father was not as frail as he looked. Ramia, I was glad. The door opened and a young girl, very fair, entered with a broom and a bucket of water.

She was good looking and quiet and appeared to be from a better class, unlike Kalu. She came close to the old man who had closed his eyes. She decided not to disturb him, but glancing at the man outside watching her, she pulled the old man's hair and asked him to get up. This pleased Kalu. He left the hall with a smile and entered the tunnel.

The old man got up and both of them smiled. She asked him to move but he refused so she changed the hay around him, sponged his body and gave him a clean dhoti. She filled the water in the pitcher after cleaning it and covered it with a clean mug. She brought out a basket and told him to hide it under the hay. He nodded. Then looking towards the tunnel and hearing voices she almost jumped and left him after locking the door. The man waited and then without opening it, threw the bundle of food through the hole and went to sleep, anticipating someone's arrival.

Two men and a woman entered – Ram Dass and Gopal with Sumitra. For a moment there was silence as Ram Dass told the woman to let him sleep. However Sumitra told Gopal to wake him up, and he bent down and pulled his beard. The man opened his eyes and looked at the woman with his large red eyes, so full of hatred, that for a moment the woman went pale. She controlled herself and asked Gopal to make him sit up.

He pulled him up roughly and asked him about his final decision. The old man didn't reply. This made Sumitra lose her temper and she said, 'Tell me the whereabouts of the family's treasure. Dhani Devi's diamond necklace and the golden statue of mother Durga you removed from the family temple.'

The man maintained his silence. Gopal pulled his hair and Sumitra kicked him as though he was an animal, but he didn't even change his expression. They tortured him further, but failed. Sumitra left the room in anger, saying it was too filthy for her to stay and that brought a smile on the old man's face. The door was closed and then there was silence all around.

I also left the room with these people and entered the secret door to the mardana, from where they entered the zenana and Sumitra Devi's room.

'You should be careful, this is the zenana and you allow everyone to enter your room,' Ram Dass warned.

'Don't worry. There won't be any separate sections for the segregation of sexes once I take over,' Sumitra replied and her eyes were shining as she looked at her husband with triumph; her husband whom she considered too weak but honest and loving.

Ramia there was silence till tea with fresh snacks were served in the room by a young girl, the one I saw in my father's room, whom Sumitra called Leela. I observed that Gopal looked at her too deeply and decided that something was cooking in his mind. They talked about the ceremony and the will and how the young heir to the haveli would be thrown out as early as possible without the villagers' knowledge, because even when Chaudhary Mohan Singh agreed to accept the forged will, people gossiped and stories against Sumitra spread far and wide – the nautchnewali who tricked the family. However, at that time they were silenced by the new Chaudhary Sahib who was under the grip of the two women and was virtually their slave.

***

Leaving her I went to the dungeon. Ramia you have been to the haveli so often and so did the older generations of your family, but none of you knew the architecture of the haveli. You only knew about my grandfather, Zoravar Singh, but not my great grandfather, Daulat Singh, and how he acquired this zamindari by deceiving the old Chaudhary, Prem Singh, and killing the entire family during the Raj.

He accused them of working against the British and that was enough. The British helped him and Daulat Singh became Chaudhary Daulat Singh at the age of twenty-one. He was the son of a poor farmer from Rampur and came to work in the haveli. He was a tall, handsome, clever man and Roma Devi, Chaudhary Prem Singh's only daughter, aged fifteen, fell in love with him.

He tried to marry her in the conventional way but the Chaudhary's family not only refused, they threw him out of the haveli which at that time had a basement and a small zenana and mardana next to the riverbed. He didn't leave the haveli and slowly started collecting hashish in the basement. Then he informed the British official at Kaurali about this and told them that the money they earned from this illegal activity was sent to the freedom fighters. This was in 1858. The British were angry and Chaudhary Prem Singh was put behind bars. His ten-year-old son, Vidya Singh was killed.

Daulat Singh married Roma Devi and became Chaudhary Daulat Singh. He was cruel, ruthless and a miser, and the people of Mauli were terrified of him. He converted the basement into a storehouse of hashish and then started the quarry with bonded labourers. Roma Devi died but no one knew how. He married his tenant's daughter, Ramoli Devi. She was young and fair, with blue eyes and chiselled features. She was uneducated but determined and bold. She changed the haveli and the cruel man – the lover of wine and women.

Ramoli Devi made him settle down and a son was born in the house of the middle-aged zamindar. Though he became a better human, what you sow you reap. He caught a venereal disease and died when he was fifty. His son, Chaudhary Gopal Singh, was only ten years. Ramoli Devi brought up her son, giving him a good moral education. No wonder Gopal Singh turned out to be a good zamindar. However, he continued smuggling hashish, but released the bonded labourers from the quarry. In short, we are not the true feudals; we acquired our blue blood through the karma of our great grandfathers. No wonder God placed these two women in the haveli to finish our family.

I reached the river and started looking around. It was hot but the labourers were still working. Then I saw two women sitting under the sun washing leaves and spreading them out to dry. They were in the same state as the quarry workers, wearing tattered saris, but they somehow looked more civilized. They were talking in whispers. One of them, called Durga, seemed to be more energetic and was calling the other 'madam'. I went close to them but couldn't place them.

Then one of them spotted Kalu coming with a whip towards them. They stopped talking and started working in earnest. He kicked the one called 'Madam' hard and threw her on the ground. He laughed and said, 'Are you my mother or Sumitra? Mother! What a laugh!' There was a silence and then he said, 'One day I shall make your daughter Leela my wife and that time is not too far.' He gave her another kick and left.

Sitting like statues, the two women watched him entering the tunnel. A bell rang and work stopped. It was just as well, because it was boiling hot. The labourers sat by the side of the two women. One of them placed a basket in the centre and distributed two dry chapattis, one onion and one green chilli to each. She placed two chapattis on some paper for the woman who was kicked by Kalu and even brought a mug of water for her.

It seemed she was different from the others. She was old but even the dirty face reflected her beauty. She was fair, with sharp features and blue eyes. She sat quietly while the others were talking filth about the nautch wali and Kalu. Durga said they were glad Beena had escaped from the quarry and they wished they could as well. The bell rang again; they cursed Kalu and rose to start work. Durga told the woman to lie down while she worked and kept an eye out for Kalu. Two hours later, after drying and packing all the leaves in a cardboard box they got up to leave. However, it was not that easy.

The man came out of the tunnel and brought more leaves. Both women started working again, because the man stood there to watch. I saw how miserable life was for these people but there was no one to lodge a complaint. I left them and crossed the river. Behind the thick bushes I saw an open space, where I found the meagre possessions of the women. Then a paper fell on me. I knew the place was below my father's room.

I was still wondering to how to pick up the paper when I heard footsteps and the women entered. One picked up the paper and gave it to the other. She said, 'The note says that Ram Dass will help both of us to be free in the near future.'

'If it is so easy why didn't he do that earlier?'

The woman lay down with a deep sigh and her eyes were misty. I went closer, and realized that she must be Leela's mother because she resembled her, except for her blue eyes. The woman called Durga helped her to sit and gave her a drink. It gave some strength and the woman thanked her.

'I don't know whether I shall live long enough to see my husband and daughter, but I must tell you my secret so that you can let the people of Mauli know after my death, how this woman Sumitra tortured me. At times I want to pardon her, but when I think of the way she treated my husband, I want her to suffer.'

Though Durga tried to silence her, the woman was too excited to stop and she told her now she wished to die rather than live like a rat in the filth. 'Durga you're Dalit but a good woman.'

***

Kanta's Story

I was the only daughter of a large landholding zamindar of the Terai. My brother who was ten years older to me adored the entire family and unlike other zamindars, we were rich and happy. The people of Shapur loved us and worshipped the haveli as the temple of kindness for the poor. I had my education at home from Indian and English tutors.

Once during Diwali, my parents and I went to Nainital where we owned a house. I was very fond of rowing, riding and swimming. This brought me close to a young man. He was my brother's classmate but had left the prestigious Taluqdar school in Lucknow before completing high school and was in Nainital to enjoy hunting with his friends. I was young, about twelve years, and innocent, but was considered the most beautiful girl in the Terai.

Chaudhary Devi Singh was a tall, handsome man with an athletic body who loved the comforts of life, wine and of course young girls. He was considered one of the most suitable feudals for marriage. We fell in love and had fun but then he received a telegram telling him to return home because his mother was ill. He promised to be back within a week. To convince me we got married in the temple. He never returned and I found myself pregnant. This created panic in my family and my brother insisted on an abortion. However I refused and one night I left my family for Mauli with my old nanny, Urmilla.

I was shocked to know that he had married Dhani Devi. There was also a rumour that the new bride was not happy and that the young man had changed, attending a nautch kotha at Kasganj. Though Nanny asked me to meet him at Mauli I refused. We had enough money so decided to settle in Lucknow. Here I had a daughter in the nursing home. I named her Leela. Then Nanny told me that my family was looking for me. So we left Lucknow and came to Kasganj. Here one day in the park, Nanny and my daughter were kidnapped. I searched everywhere, but failed to locate them. I couldn't inform the police, but during the search I was seen by the servants looking for me and thus was brought back to my parents' house.

Things settled down for a short time but they made me agree to marry the heir to Shivpuri state in east Uttar Pradesh. I refused but was forced to do so. My brother promised to search for my baby and adopt her. I got married and found my husband not only old, but intoxicated with wine and women.

The haveli was beautiful and they were rich zamindars. I had a comfortable life, but it was in the zenana and I felt like a bird in a golden cage. My brother informed me that my daughter and Nanny were in the grip of a nautch girl at Bisrauli. He brought them to Shapur and Leela started growing up there, so I was happy. Then I became pregnant and gave birth to a son whom they named Jatinder Singh. I was happy and satisfied with life. My husband was also satisfied and started leading a sedate life.

I met Chaudhary Devi Singh with Sumitra in Lucknow where we went to admit our son to junior school. I decided to ignore him but my husband and the Chaudhary became friends and later he came to dinner at our house at Shivpuri. This was the start of my misery. In spite of keeping my distance, the Chaudhary insisted on seeing me and I had to meet him. Though he gave many excuses, I was determined to lead my own life.

I discovered that Sumitra was a nautch girl and earlier a keep in his house. Though his father's wife had just died he married Savitri, a maid, but Sumitra was always with Devi Singh. Sumitra disguised herself to witness our meeting and on the third day of our return to Shivpuri, I was kidnapped.

I was tortured and starved in the dungeon and later thrown into this quarry. I don't know how many years have passed; just that I live like a rat.

There is no news of my husband and son. However I am sure this girl Leela is my daughter but who will confirm it?

***

The woman was exhausted and as she tried to stand up, she lost consciousness. I felt sad and though there was no time to help her, I knew she would be out soon. Ramia, God is great he has given so much to cruel people like Sumitra, but very little help to the innocent ones. You may say this is because of karma, but I differ being sure that I will also suffer in the next birth.

I was about to leave when a man and woman entered. They were Leela and Ram Dass in disguise. Durga was busy with the sick woman, and they approached the two. Ram Dass whistled and the old vaid from the village came out from behind the bushes. Ramia I was now sure she would live, because this vaid is renowned. He felt her pulse and gave her a powder.

She opened her eyes and looked around. Ram Dass whispered something in her ear and this brought some life into her. She tried to stand, but he stopped her and signalled to Leela to come closer. The girl held the woman and both cried. I was convinced that Leela was her daughter.

Sumitra used Kalu to torture Kanta, but he is not her son. I am glad that my father will live with her till death parts them.

They told Durga to look after her and left in a hurry through the bushes. For the first time I saw this woman smiling while holding Durga's hand.

I decided to meet you Ramia. I wish to stay for one more day, so pray for me and I am sure Lord Krishna will listen to my plea.

Now it is dawn and I must go to see the ceremony being

performed. This will be Ram Dass' day, and tonight will see the exit of these two women. If I am still here, I shall tell you before I leave so for now I must say good bye.

Ramia don't cry. Just pray for Chaudhary Mohan Singh's soul to remain on this earth for another twenty-four hours.

The Thirteenth Day

I ARRIVED AT THE haveli. The hall was clean and my photograph was placed in the centre. Carpets were spread on the floor, leaving some empty space for the pandit. It was the thirteenth day after my death and the ceremony was to be performed to begin my journey and prepare the way to Lord Yama's kingdom.

It was dawn and people started entering the haveli. Some of them asked why the ceremony was held so early in the morning. The reply, given in whispers, was that the two women wished to get rid of everyone, even the young master, the future heir and owner of the haveli, Chaudhary Gujral Singh. Some sighed and others smiled, but most were angry at the injustice to the young man and were not happy.

The gathering of the locals was complete by the time the clock struck nine. I looked at Sumitra, so old, yet even now one of the best actresses and my eunuch wife in a pure white silk sari sitting next to my clean-shaven handsome son. The new young pandit Gopal, so treacherous and a slave of these women, enjoying my money; I felt literally sick and helpless.

The pandit Gopal, son of a butcher, now sat in front of my photograph on the raised cushioned pedestal. He lit the earthenware lamp and placed flowers and burning incense in front of it. Then he marked a white circle around it. According to Hindu belief it represented the body of a preta, a dead man. The circle constitutes an umbilical cord through which the soul of the deceased can consume the ritual offerings.

These thirteen days following the funeral ceremony are dedicated to the formation and development of a thumb-sized body of the soul by means of the ritual feeding. Each of these days corresponds to a lunar month ending with birth in the world of the soul's ancestors, from where the soul of the deceased entered a new condition of existence. It acquires a body with a sheath which on this day is shed. This is similar to a snake which is born with a sheath, and when it sheds it, a new life of growth starts. Such a metamorphosis takes place in the human soul. Soon after the pindya pitra yojnas on the thirteenth day, the soul acquires the embryonic body of the preta, ready to grow and leave this world for its transmigration.

My son sat on a separate mat, close to the pandit. There was a third mat placed on the side, representing Lord Vishnu's presence, which is invoked by placing dhurba leaves (grass) on it. Ten balls made of barley, flour, sesame seeds, sugar, milk, yogurt, butter and milk were placed inside the circle. The balls are called pindas.

The pandit explained the reason for this ritual, which is to provide the deceased soul with a body. An invocation was repeated while placing a sweet on each ball and arranging them inside the circle. For the first pinda he recited: 'May this form the head'. The second, the neck and shoulders; the third, fourth, fifth and so on formed the heart, chest, back, abdomen, stomach, groin, intestines, legs, ankles and feet. Finally, the priest followed this with a supinda of the deceased and said, 'May this give birth to nutrition and satisfy hunger and thirst.'

Then sets were made to the purkha (ancestors) and separated. The first set was for Lord Yama, two were for the five elements and one for the deceased, making four sets in all. Water was poured on the pindas and a long cotton thread was placed over them, weaving the different parts to create a single yatana saritra. The subtle body then received water for the first time to quench its thirst. This water was sprinkled from a shell symbolically connected with the uterus.

This ritual gesture alluded to the embryonic formation of the subtle body. Now the disembodied soul would become preta, an embryo, living as such, while waiting to be reborn. Next, the pandit recited the mantra invoking Vishnu and asking for his blessings so that the deceased is not held in hell.

The sweets were collected to be thrown into the river and the ceremony was concluded.

The pandit was offered ladoos; fresh hay was given for cows and bread for dogs who represent the infernal gods. Then my son left for the river with the pandit. A furrow was dug and the dhurba grass was laid inside. The pandit made eleven balls of rice and sprinkled them with milk and water from a shell. He invoked the names of eleven gods and asked each to quench the preta's thirst as he threw the balls into the river.

The son purified himself at home and held a feast for the priest and guests. Thus the impurity of the thirteen-days was over for the family. The priest was given a bedding, clothes, utensils, food grains and money on behalf of the deceased, and everyone departed.

Ramia, I didn't feel any change except for a fullness in the stomach as though I was hungry and had eaten.

***

Sumitra entered the young master's sitting room. He had just changed his clothes. She told him that she had arranged for the lawyer from Kaurali to be there within an hour. 'So you must eat your lunch and get ready to hear the will.'

There was no comment and this irritated the old woman. She raised her voice and said, 'From now on, learn to respect your elders and reply. I will be the last person to see any changes made by you in this haveli and my estate.'

The young man looked at her with surprise and gave a mocking smile, but without looking at him she left the room. I saw confidence on my son's face. He laughed when Ram Dass entered and said that all was well on the other side.

'What about my grandfather?'

'He is in your bedroom and Leela is looking after him.'

'And Leela's mother?'

'She is with her brother in Sudha's room. They were brought out through the tunnel. No one in the haveli knows about the raid and arrest of Kalu and the pandit,' Ram Dass explained.

'The raid on the quarry and the release of the bonded labourers who are all family members of the villagers of Mauli was carried out by the inspector during the ceremony. Kalu was surprised but had no place to hide or run. Nobody in the haveli will know till the official reading of the will. I am waiting for Kapoor, the lawyer from Lucknow.'

'You're wonderful, Ram Dass and so was my father who acted dumb for over six months, but settled everything with your help. I am sure today he will be a satisfied soul.'

The door opened with a bang and Sumitra entered with the lawyer from Kaurali who had also forged Chaudhary Devi Singh's will. The old man was just about to take out the papers when Sumitra told Ram Dass to leave so that everything was settled within the family. The young master looked at Sumitra and told Ram Dass to sit down and listen to the reading.

'How dare you talk to me in such a manner! You will ever be dependent on me,' Sumitra said fuming. The young master didn't reply. The door opened and Sneh entered but was surprised, when for the first time, the young man did not get up to touch her feet nor did her mother look at her. However in front of the lawyer she decided to keep her silence and sat next to her mother.

The lawyer took out the official papers and read that Chaudhary Mohan Singh had decided to leave everything to his step grandmother Sumitra Devi and wife Sneh. That he had already spent a lot of money on his son, so he did not require any part of the estate except what his grandmother wished to give him. However, the young man would get five hundred rupees per month, provided he left Mauli within fifteen days, never to return.

The will brought a glow on the faces of both the women. As Sumitra got up to take the paper, it was taken by the young master and he asked the lawyer who was in hurry to go, to sit down. When Sumitra asked him to apologise he ordered Ram Dass to call in the men standing outside. This confidence shocked both women and alarmed the lawyer, who sat like a statue.

Three men in civilian clothes entered and stood behind the lawyer. When Sumitra started ordering them to leave the room, the door opened and a middle-aged man entered.

'Who are you?' Sumitra asked.

'Shashi Kumar Kapoor, advocate of the High Court of Lucknow and legal advisor to the late Chaudhary Mohan Singh.'

This cast a silence in the room and both women paled. The man sat down, removed a document from his bag and started reading.

***

Chaudhary Mohan Singh's Genuine Will

I know I shall be killed by the two so-called women of my family. One is a female and the other, who calls herself the mother of my son, is a eunuch. It is strange that a eunuch can give birth to a child but she convinced me by giving me drugs.

I leave everything I own to my son Gujral Singh. Both women must be punished for their wrongdoings and they should not be allowed to take anything – cash or jewellery – from the haveli, nor should they be allowed to own any land.

My son married Nirmala, who is a very kind young woman, in Lucknow with my blessings.

I leave everything to my son and his family and am happy now that my son will bring his wife Nirmala from Lucknow to the haveli, because there will be no threat to their lives in the absence of the two women.

***

The advocate put the keys, will and a small bag in front of the young master. He declared him the master of the entire Mauli estate.

He then asked for permission to leave in order to catch the train back to Lucknow. A sudden thud made Ram Dass turn around and he saw his wife on the floor with the daughter bending down to revive her. He smiled, remembering the old days when the young Sumitra performed such acts and he would get so worried about her. He escorted the lawyer to the car near a police van where Kalu and Gopal were tied up.

People started gathering outside the haveli. Some told Ram Dass that they heard Chaudhary Devi Singh was alive and they wished to pay their respects. He nodded and entered the sitting room. What he saw satisfied him completely and Ram Dass knew the time had come for him to leave the haveli and return to Orissa.

The old man, shaved and with combed hair was clad in a white dhoti and kurta. Chaudhary Devi Singh was sitting on a chair and Leela was standing behind him. He blessed Ram Dass when he bent down to touch his feet and told him that he had to put Sumitra and Sneh under police custody. Ram Dass told him that the people of the village were outside waiting to see him. The old man, no longer looking so frail, rose and went out with Leela.

The villagers came running, bent down and paid their respects. I was happy and noticed two drops falling on the ground. I knew that I was now in the embryonic stage and the time had come for me to leave at dawn.

***

I have little time left. Look Ramia look! There is a vehicle in the sky descending to the ground. It is my mother Dhani Devi; she is calling me.

I must go but I am satisfied. Perhaps I have performed some good karma, so that instead of Yama's horrible dhoot, my mother has come to take me. It shows that she loved me and while performing charity and in her prayers, she must have requested the Lord to pardon me.

Goodbye Ramia my friend. Repeat all I have told you to a scholar so that he brings out a book for people to read and learn what happened after my death during the first thirteen days. You must give it the title 'Tervein'.

Ramia sat like a statue.

There was a sudden light on the ground and then all was dark. He bent down, touched the ground and paid his respects to the departing soul.

He was grateful that even though he was a Dalit he was chosen by the zamindar. It meant that in the other world all were the same: Dalit, Brahmin, Kshatriya, zamindar, raja and fakir; God did not differentiate between anyone and gave to each person according to their karmas. This made him smile as he entered his hut. He looked around at everything he owned and he felt inside himself that all material possessions, however meagre or large, meant nothing. He must perform good karma. If the zamindar, after all his sins, could go to heaven with such a little good karma then why couldn't he?